2 1 3

2
1
3

7 DAILY RITUALS FOR GRATITUDE

Vivida

Vivida® is a trademark property of White Star s.r.l.
www.vividabooks.com

Piazzale Luigi Cadorna, 6
20123 Milan, Italy
www.whitestar.it

This edition first published in 2024 by

Om Books International

Corporate & Editorial Office
A-12, Sector 64, Noida 201 301
Uttar Pradesh, India
Phone: +91 120 477 4100
Email: editorial@ombooks.com
Website: www.ombooksinternational.com

Sales Office
107, Ansari Road, Darya Ganj,
New Delhi 110 002, India
Phone: +91 11 4000 9000
Fax: +91 11 2327 8091
Email: sales@ombooks.com
Website: www.ombooks.com

ISBN: 978-93-53769-69-7

Printed in India

10 9 8 7 6 5 4 3 2 1

Simone Masserini

Federica Avanzi

7 DAILY RITUALS FOR GRATITUDE

Illustrations by **Riccardo Gola**

A practical guide to enjoying
every day to its fullest and to being
more self-aware

Om Books International

CONTENTS

3 Social Interaction 55

4 Family & Friends 75

5 Me Time 95

ONE SUMMER EVENING. . .

Have you ever sat at a table in a restaurant one summer evening and begun speaking with the two strangers at the table next to you? You exchange ideas and world views, and after a couple hours you go home feeling carefree and at peace? These feelings come from the discovery of something new, from broadening your perspective of new places around the world.

As you read, try to imagine us authors as those two people in the restaurant. Since we cannot have dinner with each of you readers (although we won't give up hope), we've decided to share our thirty years of research, curiosity, and experience from the field in a book. We are life partners, and what you will read here is part of a shared journey. However, any time we share something personal, we've signed our name at the top of the section.

This book is based on three important aspects: the **NUMBER SEVEN**, **RITUALS**, and **GRATITUDE**.

SEVEN is a magic number. Just type "seven meaning" into a search engine and you'll get hundreds of answers, from the world of poker to religious traditions. Here are some examples: there are seven planets we can see with the naked eye, seven colors in the rainbow, seven days in a week, the seven deadly sins and the seven cardinal virtues, seven qualities of Allah, Rudolf Steiner's seven-year cycles, lucky ladybugs have seven spots (some say it's best not to trust others), the seven *chakras*, seven musical notes, seven continents and seven oceans, Antipater of Sidon's seven wonders of the ancient world, the seven Endless from Sandman by Neil Gaiman, Snow White's seven dwarves, and seven is Harry Potter's *quidditch* number.

While writing this book, we asked each other which important seven most represents us. Simone chose the *sapta bodhyanga* (the seven factors of awakening in the Buddhist tradition, which includes mindfulness and concentration); Federica chose the perfection of human nature, which combines the four elements (water, air, earth, and fire) and the divine trinity (in Indian culture, this includes Brahma, Vishnu, and Shiva, but if you think about it, the concept of a trinity is present in many religions). In any case, *quidditch* and ladybugs almost made the final cut.

The concept of **RITUAL**, on the other hand, needs to be explained further, especially with regard to how we use it in this book.

The root of the term has distant relatives in ancient languages, from Sanskrit, in which *ri-* refers to a sense of gliding or flowing, to the Greek term *rythmos*, meaning number, and the Latin *ritus*, which has become the word rite as we know it today in religious contexts.

We have great respect for the religious rites of every type and tradition, but in this book we have chosen a more concrete interpretation. For us, a ritual is a repetitive action intended to celebrate something, and it has the necessary characteristics to become a habit.

If we think about it, all of us are already immersed in rituals: brushing your teeth every evening before bed is a ritual, as is Sunday lunch with family or brunch with friends, Friday evening drinks, or going to the gym three times a week. Pizza and beer while watching a soccer game can also be considered a ritual. These are all actions we repeat automatically that have become part of our lives and give us a sense of well-being. In this book, we have identified seven (!) moments of the day and selected seven (!) actions for each moment that we hope will become your new daily habits.

And finally, we have arrived at the heart of this book: **GRATITUDE**.

We often associate gratitude with a feeling of being affectionately thankful toward someone who has done something good for us. You most likely have strong memories associated with this feeling, whether you were the bearer or the receiver of an action that touched the heart or relieved burdens. We naturally feel grateful toward someone who has freed us of obstacles or merely simplified our life, even if just briefly.

In this book, we challenge you to introduce actions in your life that seek to achieve some sort of revolutionary gratitude. We would like to help you perceive a deeper sense of gratitude for life, yourself, and your body, which has carried you far and wide for years, a gratitude for those underappreciated, reoccurring daily moments. We challenge you to recognize how an attitude based on gratitude can be self-generated and can keep your heart open from morning to night. For us, "attitude" is a very concrete notion. It helps you focus on simple actions that can become rituals and eventually turn into good habits.

In our approach, we were inspired by a universal principle that exists in many traditions, called the Golden Rule or the Ethic of Reciprocity. This principle can be found in the words of Pittacus of Mytilene, one of the seven (!) Sages of Ancient Greece: "Whatever you rebuke your neighbor for, do not do it yourself"; in the Gospel of Matthew, in the words of Jesus: "All things whatsoever ye would that men should do to you: do ye even so to them"; in the words of the Dalai Lama: "If you want others to be happy, practice compassion. If you want to be happy, practice compassion"; and in the Torah: "Do unto others as you would have them do unto you."

We love the positivity of the Golden Rule and would like for this book to help you do for yourself what you would like others to do for you. Showing gratitude for your life and yourself positively affects others, encourages them to do the same, and little by little can help build a better world.

As you will find, we did not invent any of this. All the actions found in the book come from Western or Eastern traditions, science, pop culture, and the teachers we have either read or met in person. We put together actions and rituals we believe are accessible to everyone and tried to make each page as comprehensible as possible. We don't know if they will change your life, but we like to believe they can open your eyes to worlds you never considered before, encouraging you to take a closer look at that feeling that resonates deep in your heart.

One lesson that we have learned from experience that drives many of our choices is that although new things might be scary, they open your mind. And an open mind is the key to evolving as human beings and to becoming better people and more conscious residents of this planet.

So let's dive into this journey together! If you'd like to learn more, we've listed the authors and books mentioned throughout the book in the Notes and Bibliography section, and you can find them at your local library or bookstore, or online. There are no rules. Whatever you feel in your heart, go explore it further.

We like that what we've shared allows us to be the tools that encourage you to rekindle dormant interests. And if tomorrow you become the messengers of these rituals for others at another table in a different restaurant, the value of our book will continue to multiply indefinitely.

And since this dinner is not a monologue, we would like to know your rituals as well. Find us on social media and write us with your suggestions.

1 Awakening

According to the United Nations, human beings on an average live to be 72 years old or 26,280 days (women continue to live longer than men by about 4 years).

To generalize, let's say that we have little more than 26,000 awakenings in our life. Now, excuse me if I begin with my usual pedantic questions, but how might we include the two or three years in which we as infants simply sleep, wake, and poop? And the sleepless nights as adults spent without even touching the pillow due to partying, work, or incessant worrying? And naps? Sunday siestas? Dozing after breakfast on Sunday morning? Drifting to sleep on the beach? Intermittent passing out on airplanes and trains or any other form of transportation that's driven by someone else?

After hours of discussion, we eventually decided on 25,000 awakenings, a nice round number to make it easier to count. For those like me who already have their calculator open, that's around 68 and a half years.

So what is an awakening, where does it come from, and why is it so important to our book on rituals for gratitude that it's the first thing mentioned? We never think about it, but our lives are defined by cycles, and the sleep/wake cycle is one of the most present and most mysterious.

Sleep is a very bizarre condition in living beings. It is a typical biological aspect of the lives of many species on our planet, from elephants to humans. It divides life between dark and light (or light and dark, depending on how you approach it) and has been the subject of inquiry since ancient times.

In Greek mythology, Hypnos (sleep) and Thanatos (death) are the twin sons of Nyx (night) and Erebo (Darkness). For Romans, sleep is the place of oblivion and rest, far from the stress of real life. In Egyptian mythology, human beings had three bodies. Ka represented the "body asleep." It soared through the beyond during sleep before returning to the mortal body upon awakening.

Awakening is that sweet second between these two worlds, which is why we think it's important to start our list of rituals with this moment of your day and life.

Taking this awakening for granted is like taking the sun's rising for granted, and unfortunately we all do it and have always done it. The bad news is that when we take something for granted, it's hard to be grateful for it. In this case, we miss the chance to value that miracle that brings us back from the unknown every morning and springs us into life.

So what should we do to celebrate our gratitude for a new day?

What should we do to make every 25,000 awakenings memorable? And, not to pressure you, but if you are over 40 like us, you only have about 10,000 left. It's time you started being grateful. The good news is that many of you already do something; you're just not fully aware of it. Taking a shower (hot or cold, whatever you like) cleanses the night from us and makes the body fresh for the new day; drinking orange juice gives you a ton of vitamins and keeps your intestine happy; brushing your teeth gives you fresh breath and consistent hygiene; and meditating (for the more courageous among us) gives you the support you need to live the day better. That said, there are also less healthy habits that are worth reconsidering: skipping breakfast, watching the news, opening social media immediately after you open your eyes, or spending less than thirty minutes between bed and your car (maybe even by the time you get to the first stoplight). These are all very superficial actions but ones that could negatively influence our happiness and well-being in the long run.

Here is where we'd start our conversation in the restaurant that summer evening. Why not try beginning your day more consciously, with simple, repetitive actions that could become your beneficial awakening rituals?

Internalizing these suggestions that come from diverse traditions is not complicated at all. We hope that the simplicity of the action, along with the tradition it represents, will help you awaken with a burst of gratitude for what is essentially a miracle, the miracle of being alive, of being interconnected with everything and everyone, of having a wonderful, working body even while sleeping. In short, the miracle of life itself.

Dear Old Alarm Clock

01

FEDERICA — The title of this first ritual might be surprising. Are we really telling you to pull out an old 1970s alarm clock, as if you were in *Groundhog Day*? Searching online for the classic analog alarm clock might generate suggestions for other such objects, like hair rollers, a meat slicer, or a retro orange tube television.

Don't worry, we have no intention of taking you to Punxsutawney County in Pennsylvania on February 2 with Bill Murray. However, we would like you to join us as we reflect on the studies we began to examine to better understand how the electromagnetic waves produced by all the gadgets we (literally) take to bed might influence our sleep.

In recent years, we've found opposing opinions. Some believe that there is no scientific evidence that electronic devices can interfere with your health even at night, whereas others have demonized the use of such devices even during the day. The Food and Drug Administration (FDA) in the United States recently published a study titled *Scientific Evidence for Cell Phone*

Safety, which states that there is no "consistent or credible scientific evidence of health problems." Therefore, we have decided to make it a matter of common sense. At night, do we really need to hear or see notifications for some useless newsletter we are subscribed to? Or comment on the latest wild night out of an ex-boyfriend from high school? Do we really need to check that pancake recipe?

Honestly, no, you really don't. So, why not leave your phone charging in the kitchen or some other room and put an alarm clock next to your bed, an object that serves one purpose only: to wake you up at a set time. One of my Buddhist teachers always said: "If you have a strong desire to eat chocolate and you can't resist it, start with the first logical response. Stop buying chocolate."

If we physically distance ourselves from our addictions, including late-night likes, notifications, and updates, we probably won't completely free ourselves of them; but in the meantime, our dreams are undisturbed and we awaken better. Whether electromagnetic waves from our devices influence the quality of sleep or not, before the year 2000 human beings successfully woke up like this every morning!

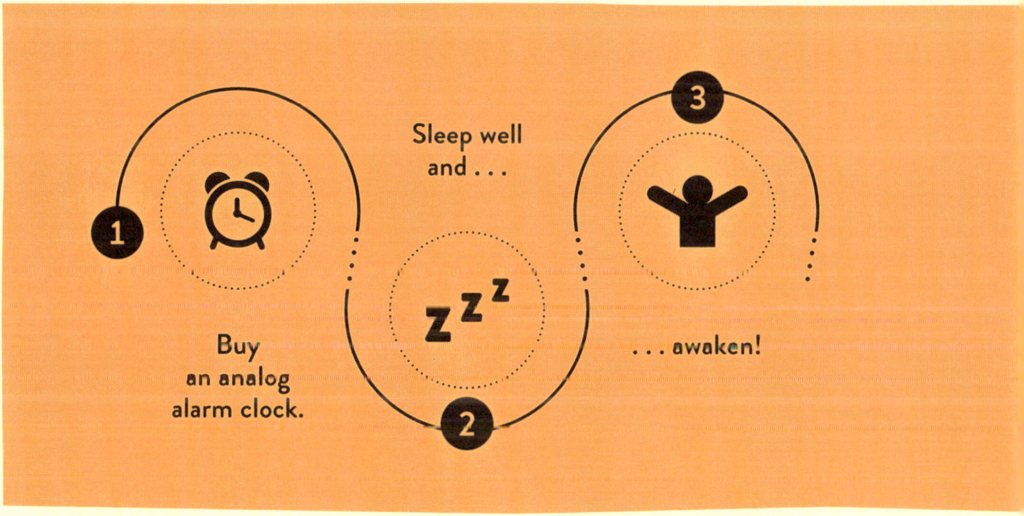

As Easy as Drinking Water

02

SIMONE — For many years, I lived with my grandmother, and I affectionately remember how she used to lean against the kitchen sink in her nightgown in the morning and sip a glass of lukewarm lemon water. Back then, I didn't understand what she was doing—and I'm not sure she fully did either. It was probably a habit she picked up from her family.

In recent years, what I thought was just one of my grandmother's habits started popping up on the websites of pop culture magazines and daily newspapers alike. Anthony William, author of the bestsellings books *Medical Medium*, wrote about it exhaustively in his book on the liver, divulging evidence of the hydrating and cleansing power of lemon water. His very unconventional diet and meditation rules greatly helped us explore a different perspective on several topics. Let's get back to the water (which you should drink at least thirty minutes before breakfast), a practice that is also found in Ayurvedic tradition, the ancient Vedic science, which claims it stimulates gastrointestinal reflexes and facilitates morning bowel movements to finalize your digestion from the night before.

Ancient Japanese culture also suggests drinking at least half a liter of water with lemon and ginger right after waking up to rehydrate your body, which worked all night with no food or water. I don't think my grandmother knew about the principles of Ayurveda or Anthony William, but for her whole life she spent the first five minutes of her day sipping a glass of water with lemon, looking out of the window as the shadows of night made room for the day.

When I drink my half liter of water with lemon in the morning, I think of her, and it warms my heart. I don't know if it's the free radicals or if it's just in my head; but ever since I started this ritual, my days begin better. That's why I recommend trying it for yourself. After all, it's as easy as drinking water!

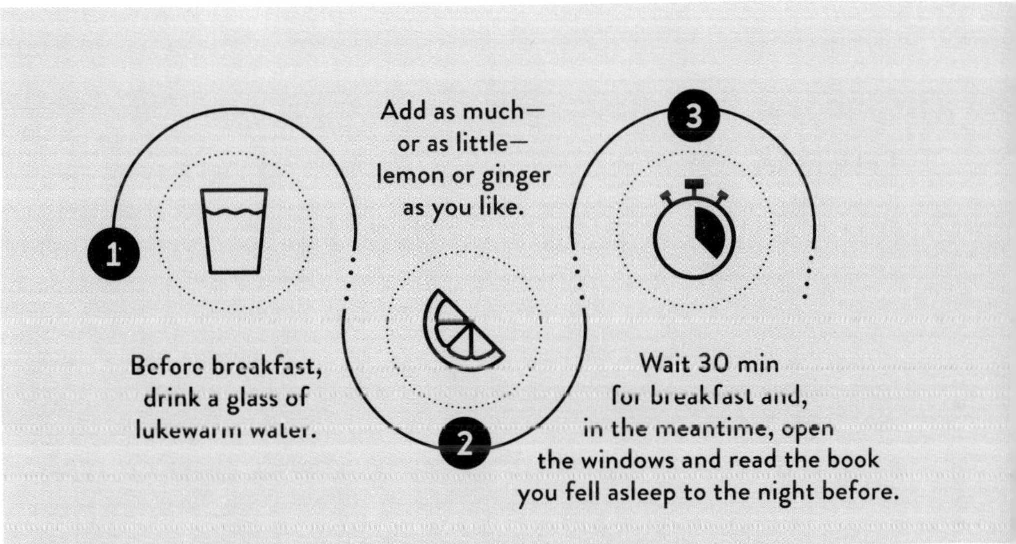

Tongue Scraping and Oil Pulling

03

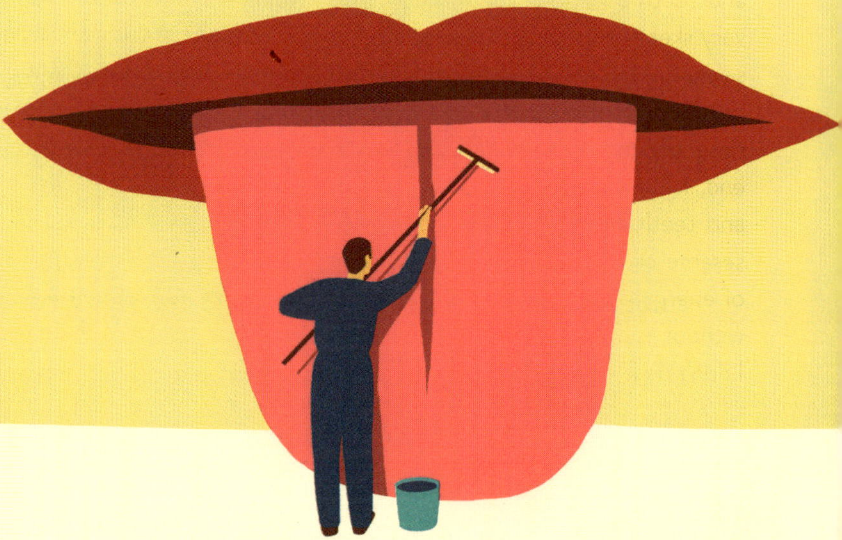

FEDERICA — The sweet taste of awakening is not always so sweet, especially if you spent a wild night out the night before. As we already mentioned, there's a deep and concrete connection between an awakening and everything from the day before. As someone who does yoga, I've always appreciated the morning practices of Ayurveda. This ancient discipline, whose practices are sometimes debatable but generally enjoyable, dedicates the first part of an awakening to internally and externally cleansing the body. We Westerners believe we wake up clean, but our bodies have just spent 6 to 8 hours busily working to complete digestion and to transform, regenerate, and build "things" inside of us. Ayurvedic rituals start here, cleaning and awakening the energy in our bodies. The first step is a glass of lukewarm water (no lemon for me, thanks) to stimulate and finish what began with dinner the night before, because before starting anything, waste is "better out than in," as Shrek says.

Then it's time to clean the tongue and teeth and do an oil pulling. I was very skeptical the first time I tried this, saying "My tongue is clean" and "I brush my teeth after breakfast" and "I will not rinse my mouth with oil!" But in the end, I found that brushing my tongue and teeth and rinsing my mouth with sesame oil first thing gives me a burst of energy. Today, years later, I can't go without it. I even feel out of sorts when I don't do it.

I don't know if this energy comes from the practical gesture or the energetic gesture, but starting my day like this is both a moment of awareness and purely a pampering. I thank Ayurveda every morning for this routine!

An ancient Indian saying says that "Those who clean the tongue, clean the heart." The oral cavity and tongue are directly connected to your ability to express yourself and your world through words.

This ritual helps us start our day with a clean tongue and a heart full of energy! Then, after breakfast, we brush our teeth with toothpaste.

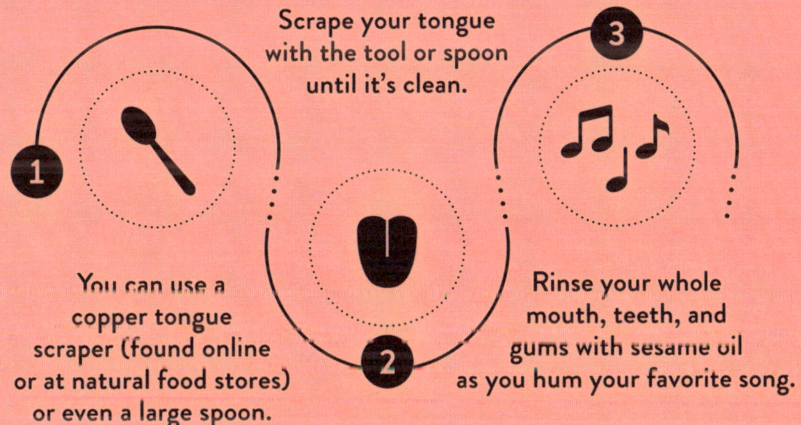

Make Your Bed!

04

FEDERICA — When it comes to sleep, no one is better at it than me! I know I'm very lucky. I can fall asleep in a heartbeat, and when I wake up, I'm fully awake. I have this sort of ON/OFF switch (which Simone envies and he would like to know where he can find one). The rare nights in my life that I struggled to sleep, I could tell you exactly why; it's usually due to an uncomfortable bed. Therefore, I am maniacally picky about my pillow and mattress. Some time ago, during one of my creative spurts, I wholeheartedly wanted to thank the inventor of the mattress in my evening prayers. Like usual, I started doing some research online.

It wasn't as easy as I expected. For some reason, I thought I'd find some genius inventor from the eighteenth-century French court, a certain Jean Jacques Materasse or similar, the first to have the brilliant idea of covering something with wool to make sleeping a pleasurable experience for the body.

Instead, as was to be expected, not only had prehistoric humans already come to this conclusion (according to research by archaeologist Lyn Wadley from the University of Witwatersrand in Johannesburg), but it seems that every morning they would also reconstruct their bedding of stems, reeds, and compacted leaves—specifically the Cryptocarya woodii—for the following night.

Therefore, the practice of remaking the bed every morning is ancient. This reminds me of Admiral William McRaven, who gave a brilliant speech at the University of Texas in 2014, in which he says that making your bed and fixing your pillow can be your first goal for the day, and once you've done this, everything else is easier.

This simple and powerful gesture can affect the mood of your day. So, c'mon! Make your bed! Whatever your philosophy—anthropological or military—this is an excellent morning ritual. Don't leave your duvet wrinkled, pajamas thrown about haphazardly, sheets messy, and a pillow that still shows the shape of your head the whole day. I don't know how productive this will make you, but when you return to your orderly and welcoming bed, you will certainly thank yourself for starting your day with this ritual.

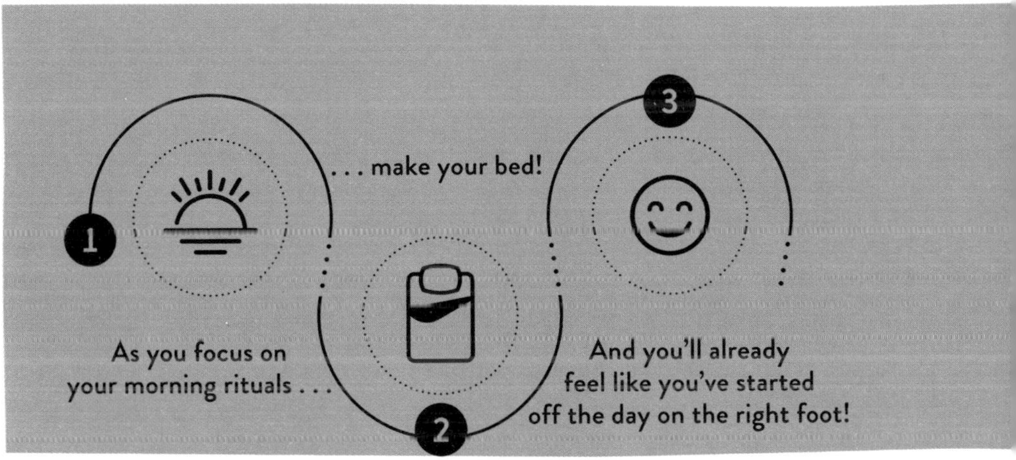

A Digital-Free Start to the Day

05

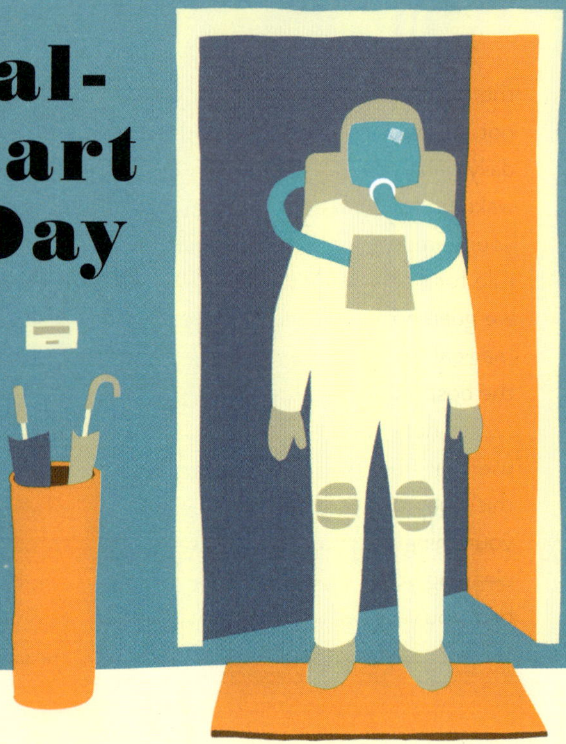

SIMONE — I've spoken often with impassioned advocates of the digital detox, which encourages you to disconnect from the Internet, social media, and your phone in general for 24, 48, or 72 hours, depending on the approach. Those who've done it claim its benefits are miraculous. Some said they finally slept like a baby, others that they finally spent time reading a book (some even two!). The most enthusiastic people even found time to "really" speak with friends and family. However, I've always been skeptical of this "cold-turkey"-for-a-limited-amount-of-time method.

I instead suggest taking a "middle way," like the Buddha describes in his first sermon in the Deer Park of Sarnath, near Varanasi, India, as he conceived the Noble Eightfold Path. The Buddha, who had transcended two extreme life styles—his first twenty-nine years as a prince and the next six of extreme asceticism, invites those who seek a stable, lasting, and conscious path to choose The Middle Way.

It might be tempting to renounce the digital world for 72 hours, but why not instead try adopting the simple, daily habit of waiting an hour after you wake up to look at your phone, turn on your computer, or watch TV? It's been a rule for Federica and me for years, and we guarantee that a slow exit from the magical world of our dreams is one of the best moments of our day.

I'm not necessarily saying you should use that hour to do all of the rituals in this chapter, since they might not be your thing (although between drinking, cleaning your tongue, and making your bed, you've almost done them all). What I mean is to appreciate an easy return to reality without immediately flooding your mind with information.

For many, an hour is not much. If you want to understand how much time we spend on social media, read the analysis from Broadband Research. No one can prevent you from spending two hours looking at the lives of others on social media or reading the news online, but I suggest at least starting your day "free" of devices, screens, and information and dedicating some time to yourself before being thrown into the deafening, chaotic jungle of the digital world.

You've Got Mail

06

SIMONE — Ever since I can remember, there were always paper notes left on the kitchen tables of the houses I grew up in. They contained a mix of information and messages of different types from the first to wake up, who was also usually the first to leave, to everyone who would wake up later. "I'll drive past the bakery and get bread" was often written next to "Wish aunt Gina a happy birthday today," "Be good for grandma," and "Have a good day." Over the years, the to-dos slowly became less frequent, but the practice of leaving notes remained. I carried on the tradition in my own life with Federica. However, I now use masking tape, which is more fun since I can put it anywhere she might go.

When my parents became empty-nesters, the tradition softened; instead of instructional messages, they wrote affectionate and sweet love notes. Something my dad does that I've always found sweet and that I've never had the courage to correct him on is his use of the word SMECK, an incorrect Anglicism (smack, like a kiss) that came to have special meaning for my mother. In the final years of her life, it was more and more present, both in frequency and in the size of the letters.

Getting back to our rituals, every book about professional and personal efficiency has many references to these types of notes. In many cases, they are part of the daily "to-do list" category. All these books say the same thing: "If you want a successful life, you must have a clear to-do list: first this, then this, and if you have time"—and you should have time, otherwise you were efficient enough—"do also this and this and this." These books also tell you when to write your to-do lists. Some say the night before, like writer, illustrator, and coach Alex Mathers, and others, like time-management expert Laura Vanderkam, say before breakfast.

We'll let the others tell you what's the most effective daily routine. We're just here to suggest adding a few words of affection to your "messages" for yourself and the people near you, maybe even with a few errors that become part of the love language of your family, whoever that might be for you. When you find them years later, surely you'll have forgotten WHAT you had to do that day, but you'll remember WHO you wrote it for.

So, let me end this chapter with a nice message for you, written by hand in memory of my father—SMECK!

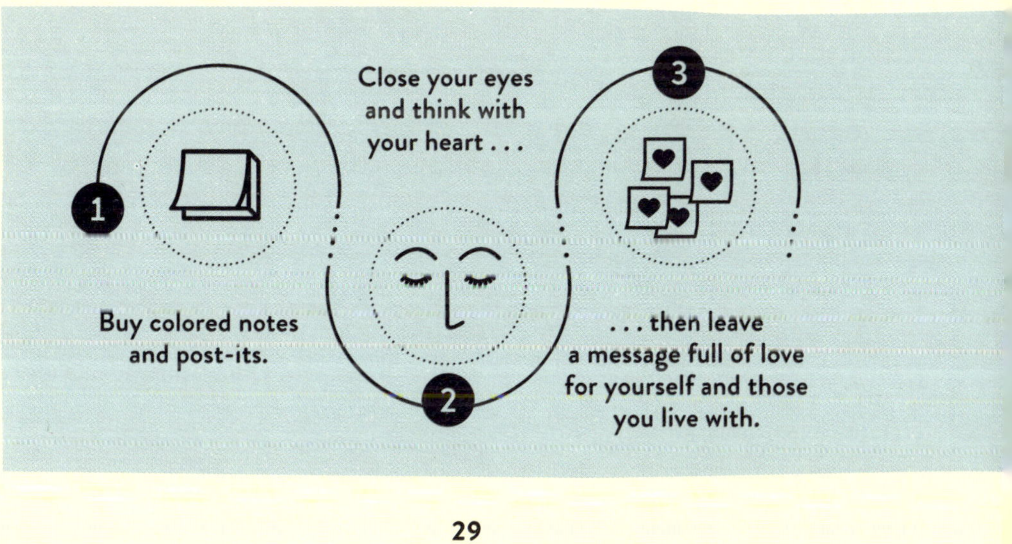

An Angel Card a Day

07

SIMONE — The Findhorn Foundation is a magical place in northern Scotland, where I was lucky to spend some time several years ago. It was "unintentionally" founded in 1962 and is still today a global center for those who seek an interior and alternative spiritual path. The members of the Findhorn Foundation have developed many tools from their more than fifty years of experience, which they still use for their public seminars.

Some of my favorite tools are the Angel Cards designed by Joy Drake and Kathy Tyler. The Angel Cards are actually part of the Game of Transformation, a type of board game in which, instead of passing GO and collecting

200 dollars like in Monopoly, you embark on a journey to discover a deeper part of yourself. The 72 cards don't depict actual angels, but rather words that represent the numerous qualities of an angel.

Compassion, abundance, friendship, grace, adventure, and fraternity are just some of these. Every morning, Federica and I fish one out of a bowl before leaving the house, and we let the word guide us through our day.

It's a simple ritual that takes only a few seconds, but it's interesting how in the middle of a work meeting about some project deadline, suddenly the angel of patience I fished that morning pops up. These moments of meaningful coincidence, which Carl Jung would define as synchronicity, are valuable because they reconnect us to the present. In those moments, the chosen word gives us a choice: we can be rigid and insist that things be done by the established rules, or we can take a deep breath and find another path.

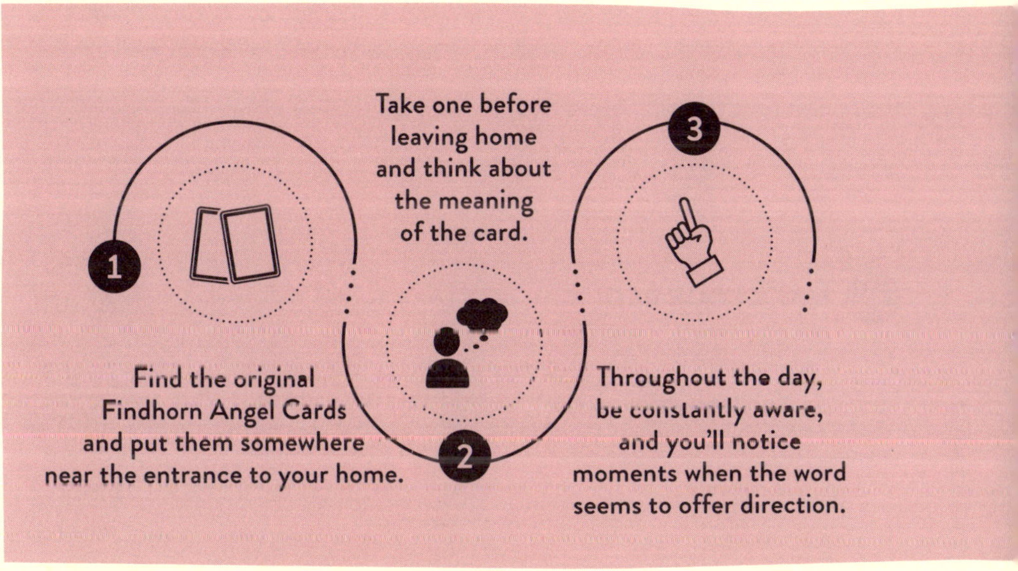

Notes and Sources

01 DEAR OLD ALARM CLOCK. We are often unable to give ourselves limits, so we transform the freedom to do what we want into toxic habits. The Buddhist teacher Khenpo Mirti explains this in his lessons at the Karmapa International Buddhist Institute (KIBI) in New Delhi. If we cannot contain our incorrect desires, then we must begin to do the simplest thing, which is to distance ourselves from anything that might make them worse.

---

02 AS EASY AS DRINKING WATER. A good friend of ours told us about Anthony William, the "Medical Medium," over dinner. Since we didn't know him, we bought his book *Liver Rescue*. Reading it was an important watershed moment for us, and we found many benefits in some of his suggestions. If he interests you, we suggest starting with the book *Medical Medium*.

---

03 TONGUE SCRAPING AND OIL PULLING. One of my favorite volumes about Ayurveda is *The Idiot's Guide to Ayurveda* by Sahara Rose Ketabi with an introduction by Deepak Chopra, a hugely successful book. It is a simple but complete book on a subject that is, needless to say, very complex. It explores not just the ancient science of life according to the Vedas, but also a more general way of understanding human beings and our illnesses and imbalances. Ayurveda lovingly recreates the marvel that we are as human beings and as part of the universe.

---

04 MAKE YOUR BED! When we read more, we discovered how useful the *Cryptocarya woodii* is. This small African tree has insecticide and bug-repellent properties that are excellent for keeping unwanted critters away at night. In the video of Admiral McRaven, his speech begins "If you want to change the world, start off by making your bed." It's six minutes long. Like the admiral, we believe that starting with the little things is the magical key to everything.

---

05 A DIGITAL-FREE START TO THE DAY. There are many books that talk about the Noble Eightfold Path of the Buddha. However, these types of books should be read alongside some sort of annotation, or else they're hard to understand. We suggest *The Heart of the Buddha's Teaching*, annotation by Thich Nhat Hanh. If, however, you want to know more about the Land of Dreams and how its Lord created it from magical sand, we recommend getting lost with Neil Gaiman in his masterpiece comic *Sandman*. And yes, you can read it while eating breakfast. Lastly, for statistics about the use of social media, check out the following link: www.broadbandsearch.net/blog/average-daily-time-on-social-media

06 YOU'VE GOT MAIL. We don't have the notes Simone's parents would leave, but the *7 Daily Rituals* Instagram profile sometimes shares those that Simone leaves for Federica.

07 AN ANGEL CARD A DAY. Go explore the website of the Findhorn Foundation to find out about the original Angel Cards and to visit the wonderful section called Daily Inspiration.

2 Eating

Eating is an integral part of our lives. This seems obvious because as children we are taught that "an empty bag cannot stand upright" (as my grandma and probably other grandmas would say). But in this second chapter, we would like to focus on making you aware of something that goes beyond popular wisdom and common sense.

When we talk about eating, we must understand what we're actually talking about. We might be referring to the three meals a day, breakfast, lunch, and dinner. But what about those who skip breakfast because they are in a hurry or simply aren't hungry? Or those who just have a coffee until lunch? Can eating a sandwich while on the phone be considered a meal? Can we compare an English breakfast of eggs, sausages, mushrooms, and beans to the typical Italian cappuccino and pastry? Is a French *croissant* better or worse than a Spanish *churro*?

These questions prove that defining daily meals is not so obvious. In the Western world, the average person lives to around 72 years old and consumes a little less than 79,000 "meals."

However, this doesn't take into consideration the milk we drink from our mothers as infants, a 24/7 restaurant, and the breakfasts that become lunch or just a snack for night owls. One thing is sure, though: Food is constantly present throughout our day.

We manage this presence in many different and imaginative ways depending on our nature and where we are in life. Food is a part of survival but also an expression of ourselves, a sense of social belonging, a symbol of conformity or rebellion.

But let's not get ahead of ourselves. If you're paying attention, you'll notice that we are surrounded by food, displayed everywhere like the beautiful and persuasive sirens of Ulysses.

At home, we have pantries full of food because "you never know." If you walk down the street, you can smell the fresh pastries and warm bread of bakeries. Supermarket shelves are stacked high with thousands of different types of food, and then there are restaurants, which are often lined up one after the other on city streets. And if that weren't enough, cities are teeming with vending machines that serve as little islands of urban sustenance. Perhaps you're leaving work in the evening when you're hit with a pang of hunger and want a tuna sandwich. You can stop and get one, fresh and ready to eat, from these anonymous hotspots, just thirty minutes before you get home and sit down for dinner.

Creativity reigns supreme in offices. Some have kitchens with a couple of fridges that host containers of every size and color that are regulated by strict rules: All employees must write their name clearly on the container and remember to remove whatever is left Friday evening. Then there are offices full of vending machines, again with the cold and anonymous aspect of those found throughout the city. Others might offer an attentive and obsessive selection of organic, sugar-free, and gluten-free options. And finally, there are offices that, in the absence of cafeterias, kitchens, and machines, relegate mealtime to the local cafe outside the office. These places often create an unexpected separation from the office, with the advantage of not having to pay rent.

Not even transportation areas and places where we spend short amounts of time are immune to the excess of food. Think about the gym, where we might go once or twice a week. How many energy bars and energy drinks does it have to offer? Then there are cinemas with their hot popcorn and walls of gummy candy and theaters with bars to prevent pre-, during-, and post-show pangs of hunger. In this part of the world, food is everywhere, and it's impossible not to confront its presence.

Going back to the concept of "our" daily meals, how might we define them? Nibbles, breaks, snacks, big breakfasts, quick lunches, light dinners? Finding an answer is difficult. There are too many options, too many variables, too many habits connected to food. With the next seven rituals, we will attempt to look at this subject with different eyes, connecting food to something deeper and examining it without judgment: for example, we won't address whether we should be fruitarians, raw-food eaters, omnivores, etc. It doesn't matter to us *what* you eat, so we won't preach about it. We care about *how* you eat.

What do we miss when we don't pay attention to the act of eating? We are lucky, and we care that this luck, this abundance, these opportunities are not wasted.

Many places around the world today still don't have abundance; but if we focus on feeling guilty, we won't get very far.

Instead, with gratitude and awareness, we can dedicate love and attention to these daily moments—if we really put our heart into it—and develop a shared sense of communion with others and the universe, which shows a concrete appreciation for what we have.

The Journey of a Carrot

01

SIMONE — Have you ever picked vegetables from a garden, brought them inside, washed them, and they were ready to eat in less than ten minutes and twenty meters? I have, during summers in the countryside with my Aunt Maria. It was a daily ritual, but only now do I recognize how fortunate we were for this.

Today, seasonal food that's available year-round has distanced us from these simple gestures, like that of picking an apple from a tree, wiping it on your shirt, and biting into it there in the shade of the tree. How can we reconnect to the food we find on our plates? Some years ago, in Jan Chozen Bays's book *Mindfulness on the Go*, a series of suggestions for how to maintain awareness, we came across an easy exercise that fits perfectly into these reflections. In short, the author suggests we think about the food on our plates and try to imagine the whole supply chain and every person, element, and interaction that it passed through to get to us in that moment. Let's start with an easy food: the carrot in the salad we might order at a restaurant. The supply chain of this carrot might seem easy to trace: someone planted it, someone harvested it, someone else washed and plated it, and it ended up on the table in front of us. Simple, no? However, let's look a little deeper. We realize that someone also had to water it, fertilize it, and transport it and that the trucks that transported it had to be fueled by gas stations and, first, built in factories.

Approaching it this way, it's easy to get off track. And you might be wondering: Why are we racking our brains over a carrot? It's simple: We owe all those people behind the scenes huge thanks. Gratitude for what we have is the fulcrum for being better, more-aware people. And it can all start with a carrot.

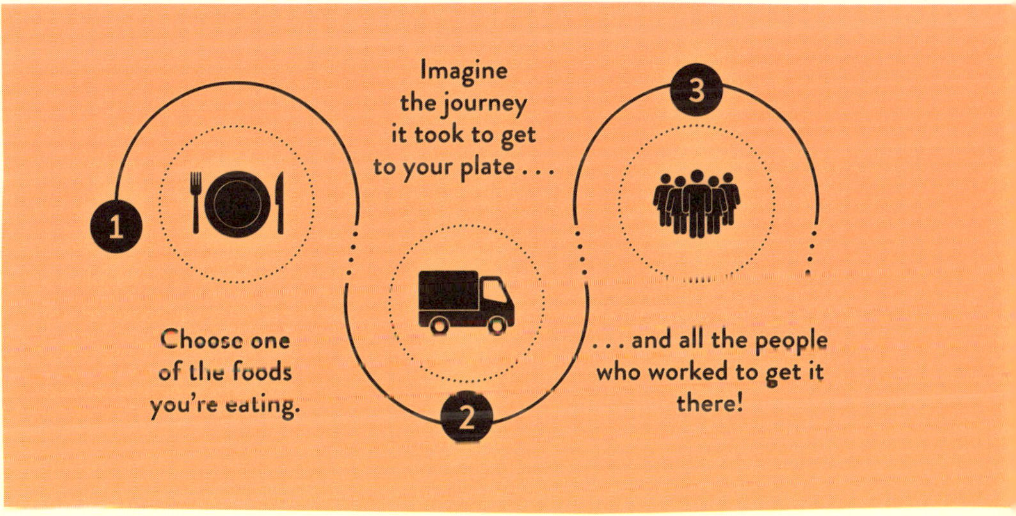

Popular Wisdom and Modern Science

02

FEDERICA — I consider popular sayings to be an expression of universal truth. Regardless of where they come from, these sayings can be fun but are, more importantly, almost all very true. One of my favorites is a saying from the great philosopher and medieval doctor Moses Maimonides, who said "Eat like a king in the morning, a prince at noon, and a peasant at dinner." I like it because I love breakfast, am fine with lunch, and hate dinner.

A specific personal memory is probably what fostered my love of breakfast. When I would spend vacation in the mountains as a child, my father would get up before everyone and would go get fresh bread, warm cookies, cheeses, marmalades, eggs, and some speck, and when I woke up I would find a table full of fresh, healthy, and delicious foods!

In 1729, Jean-Jacques Dortous de Mairan, although he was probably not as connected to the morning as I am, was the first person to discover the existence of the endogenous circadian rhythm, a sort of complex internal clock that is synchronized with the natural cycle of the day and night through natural and social stimuli (for example, having lunch at the same time every day).

His studies were carried on by Professor Joseph Takahashi at the University of Texas Southwestern Medical Center, where he studies how genetics and molecular medicine are the basis of circadian rhythms and how these even influence our metabolism, liver, and daily performance.

It would seem that following these rhythms not only helps our body but also allows us to defeat anxiety that might attack when "something" is wrong due to eating too much or too little. Isn't this what we do with our car as well? We take care of it, are grateful for it, and let it sit in the garage when necessary.

Chewing Water and Drinking Food

03

SIMONE — For years, I lived in a house with a large painting on the living room wall. It was a giant semicircle that contained the names of almost all the foods we consume regularly. I remember how confused I felt, trying to understand why sugary drinks were on the left, red meat was on the right, and whole-grain rice was in the middle. That painting was my introduction to macrobiotic food, for which I have Francesca to thank. At the time, she was my girlfriend, and she used the semicircle to teach others how to cook with balance, harmonizing the *yin* and *yang* of our lives. Macrobiotics is a broad subject. The Notes section contains many resources that will open up a whole world. According to the father of Macrobiotics, Georges Ohsawa, what keeps the world going is the balance between these two forces; and with this in mind, we must think about the food we eat and our lives in general.

I would like to share a habit that serves as one of the first rules of macrobiotics and has become a part of our lives without much difficulty. It is an easy but very effective ritual that is roughly translated as "chew water and drink food." Essentially, the idea is that we chew our food very well, even water, following the general rule of 30 chews per bite. I've always interpreted this number as more of an invitation to slowly taste our food, an easy, ready-to-use tool for paying attention to what we are doing, or eating, without distractions that make me swallow without realizing it.

Over the years, I have discovered that chewing consciously is something very dear to Thich Nhat Hanh and his followers, because paying attention to chewing connects us to the deepest part of ourselves. We can see it as a sort of active meditation, one of the many tools we can use to recenter ourselves, allowing us to be grateful for the food we have and often take for granted.

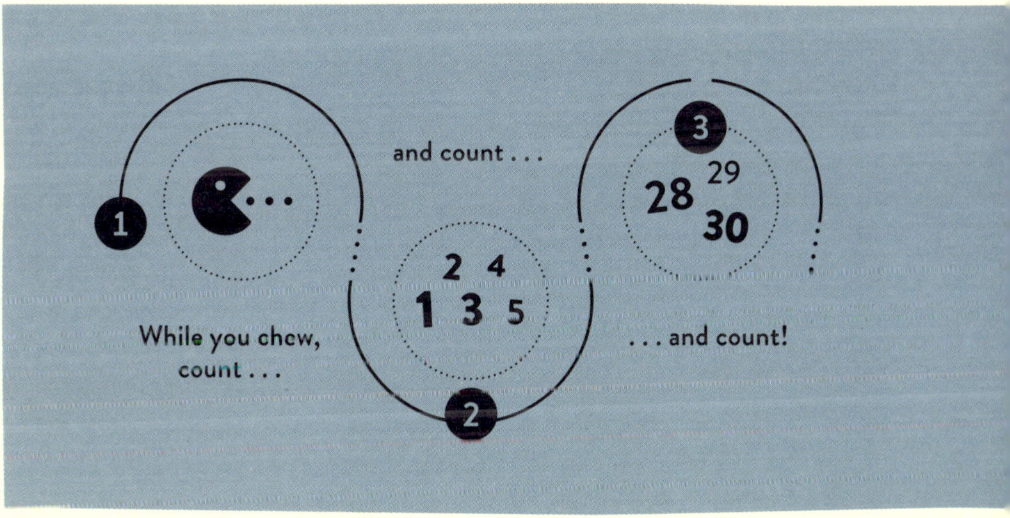

A Day Without

04

FEDERICA — When I work late in the evenings, I sometimes eat an entire bar of dark chocolate without even realizing it. One square at a time, I treat myself to compensate for the frustration of having to return to the computer after dinner. In reality, after a few squares, my stomach is full, and I realize that I'm no longer eating chocolate but just mechanically repeating the gesture of eating chocolate. I would also like to ignore this feeling because, this evening, I deserve it; so please go away!

The same sensation also brings my attention to the glass of wine I shouldn't have had, the extra forkful I should have left behind, the slice of strudel that I could have avoided. I am deeply convinced that we already harbor this awareness inside us; however, we are lazy and don't listen to that voice deep down that tells us how to work to our advantage rather than creating difficulty. We perceive this feeling but then we always find a reason to continue doing what we do. We tend to use logic because it seems primitive to trust our instincts.

One trick that helps me is to distance myself from food and drinks that I believe I abuse. But for how long? For me, as long as it takes to return to a state of consciousness and gratitude. Ten years ago, believing it was wrong to eat animal protein, I stopped eating it for one week a month and would only eat cereals, legumes, vegetables, and fruit. I applied the same theory to coffee at a time when I drank too much (and decided to go without one day a week), then I did the same with refined sugar.

Staying away from my "food abuses" helps me reclaim gratitude for those foods, which are not bad in and of themselves but become bad through superficial behavior.

What's in the Fridge?

05

FEDERICA — We don't always have time to shop for food as often as we would like, and sometimes we open the fridge to find a strange collection of leftover food: three fennels, a sad bulb of garlic, a dwindling jar of anchovies, a lemon, and a jar of capers . . . The sight of this is discouraging, especially after a long day. I always want to send a message to Simone, saying "Delivery tonight?" But we've set down some rules, and this isn't the solution! So I use what I know best: creativity. I start playing around and imagine how the different foods might go together. "Of course," my friends might say, "it's easy for you. You know how to cook." But that's not what I'm depending on. I can do it because I'm not afraid to mess up and because I'm not good at following recipes! But it's true that I lovingly take risks, then I find a name for my creations, like *Fennel au Gratin at the Bottom of the Sea* in this case.

During the 2020 lockdown, I admiringly watched Massimo Bottura's Kitchen Quarantine Instagram video series. The Michelin-starred chef would make meals for his family using what he had on hand in his house. Of course, he has a professional pantry, but I did identify with his playful way of approaching cooking.

If you shift the focus from having a specific craving and accept working with what you have, you will not only have fun but also avoid food waste, transforming the experience into gratitude!

Consider these statistics: Around a third of the food in the world goes to waste, or 1.6 billion tons, which is about 51 tons a second. I don't think anyone likes throwing food away, so why not play around with what's in the fridge and use everything we have, challenging ourselves to not throw anything out. Let's invent and create some Chef Gratitude recipes, thanking our fridge because it's not empty.

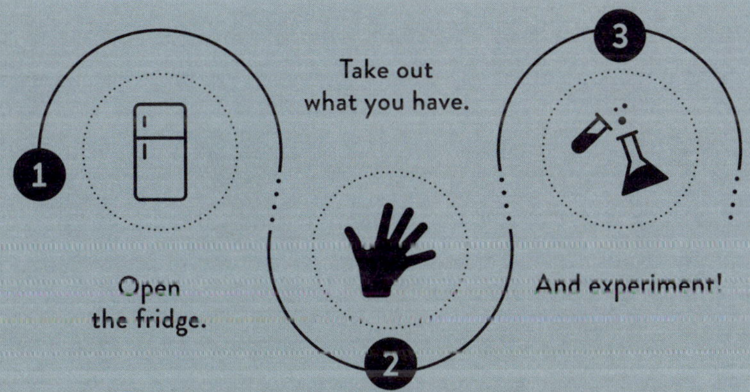

Hara Hachi Bun Me

06

FEDERICA — Ah, Confucius! Philosophy is teeming with practical gestures, unlike what most people tend to think! "Hara Hachi Bun Me" is a Confucian teaching that roughly means "Eat until your stomach is 80 percent full." Japanese Zen and Ayurveda draw inspiration from this principle to express the same concept: stop eating just before you are full. "Hara Hachi Bun Me" is about staying on the Middle Way and knowing how to listen to and celebrate the moment. Do you know who has mastered this knowledge? The inhabitants of Okinawa island, which has the longest-living population on the planet, thanks to this practice and their attention to food quality. Eating less does not mean letting yourself go hungry or eating sad food. It means that you recognize the feeling of fullness and can, therefore, afford better quality food because you reduce your portion sizes.

The way they set up the table in the East has always fascinated me. They pay great attention to the aesthetics with all the little plates, bowls, and platters that look like they came from a dollhouse. This visual component enhances the experience of eating. A single plate seems too simplistic in comparison, even if it's piled high with food.

Let me adapt this "Hara Hachi Bun Me" concept for us Westerners. If you can't stop at 80 percent full, try the visual experience, at least, using your aesthetic sense to help you. Pay attention to how you set up the table by dividing each food into different dishes. It might seem like a waste of time at first: "I don't have time for that!" But you will slowly realize that dividing things into small portions is just another way to be more aware of what you're eating.

This small but fun gesture will help make your table fuller and more grateful and help you understand the meaning of "Hara Hachi Bun Me."

Fasting

07

SIMONE — Many traditions use fasting in their practice. Think about Ramadan, during which Muslims don't eat or drink from sunup to sundown. Or there's the sixth precept of Mahayana Buddhism, which says you should not eat at the "wrong times." Ayurveda also suggests fasting at least twice a month during Ekadashi, the eleventh day after the new moon. Even our ancestors were used to fasting, although not for spiritual reasons. Historian Yuval Noah Harari talks about this at length in his book *Sapiens: A Brief History of Humankind*. He describes the hunter-gatherer diet that alternated between periods of abundance, when a hunt was fortunate or when fruit would be fully ripe, and long periods of fasting when the nomadic populations would move in search of more hospitable lands.

This intermittence can be seen today in many diets that mimic what was the norm in the past.

Deciding consciously to skip dinner or drink only liquids for an entire day or to eat differently on the weekend is not heroic; if you don't have any specific illness, you aren't risking your health. Think about when you skipped lunch due to an unexpected meeting last week or the dinner you couldn't make because the train was two hours late and when you got home, you went straight to bed. These unexpected events might put us in a bad mood.

We instead are suggesting that you plan them yourself. We often prefer not to eat after 4:00 in the afternoon, and we guarantee that breakfast the next morning has a different taste, not so much for the hunger but for the sense of lightness that your body and especially mind have. It's as if our entire being has taken a short vacation with all the benefits that come with it. Try it for yourself. Happily skip dinner and tune in to the sensations you feel. If you feel something new, be thankful for it, before drinking your coffee the next morning.

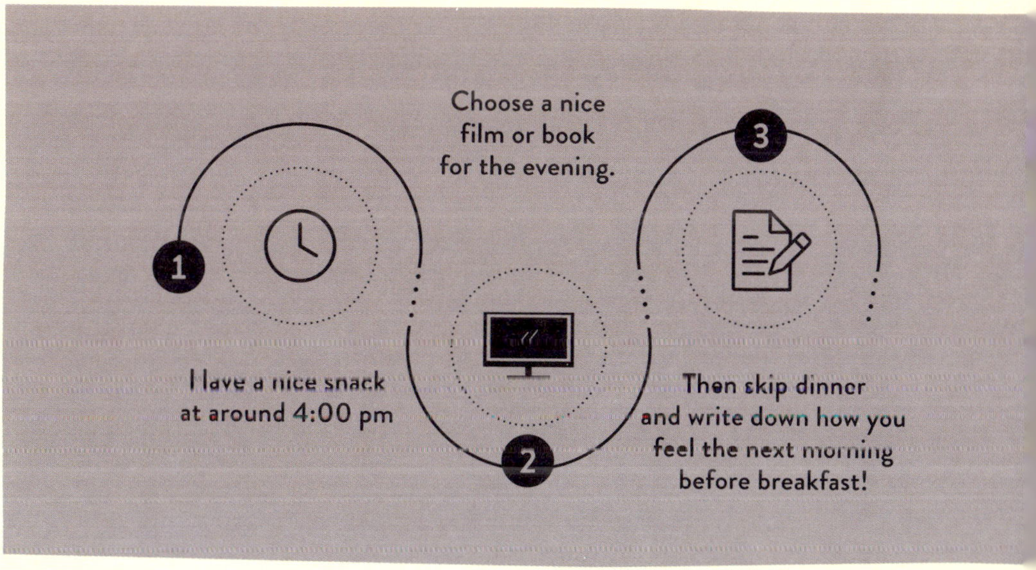

Notes and Sources

01 THE JOURNEY OF A CARROT. The Buddhist monk Thich Nhat Hanh founded a community called Plum Village in Bordeaux, France. At the monastery, one must eat in silence so that they may meditate on their food. There is a beautiful documentary on the subject by Marc J. Francis and Max Pugh called *Walk With Me*. Check it out!

---

02 POPULAR WISDOM AND MODERN SCIENCE. Carl Linnaeus, the famous botanist, designed an ideal floral clock by using species of plants that opened at different times throughout the day so that he could tell time by watching their behavior. For example, he found that dandelions would open at 6:30 in the morning, whereas other species wouldn't open until 7:00. In modern times, scientists like Joseph Takahashi are taking giant steps toward understanding the relationship we have with the matter around us. The important thing is not believing certain things, but understanding that, although we are intelligent, we are not alone on this planet, which is governed by rules far more ancient than us.

---

03 CHEWING WATER AND DRINKING FOOD. The first book we would recommend on the subject of macrobiotics is *Natural Healing through Macrobiotics* by Michio Kushi. Start here and then try to understand if this is the right path for you. It taught us so much.

---

04 A DAY WITHOUT. We have both at some point in time or another gone without certain foods for various health reasons. By listening to our bodies, we realized how beneficial it was. Thanks to a sort of hyper-instinct, we realized that when we eat too much of a certain food, eliminating it from our diet for some time can be the best solution.

---

05 **WHAT'S IN THE FRIDGE?** If you don't already have it, we suggest downloading the app "Too Good To Go," which is also our source for statistics on food waste. This Danish startup is active across almost all of Europe. It aims to save food from supermarkets and restaurants by making the food available to consumers at a lower price.

---

06 **HARA HACHI BUN ME.** One evening in Tokyo, our favorite city, we were in a *kaiseki* restaurant when our friend Hikari told us we had ordered the 15-course menu. At first, we considered canceling the order, but didn't; and by the end of the meal, the 15 little portions served in beautiful dishes that highlighted the form, color, and freshness of the flavors had left us feeling full but not stuffed! I still remember one tiny dish with *umeboshi*, salted plums, and some ginger. It was then that, in response to our questions about their way of cooking and presenting food, the kind owner explained the meaning of "Hara Hachi Bun Me."

---

07 **FASTING.** Franco Berrino is an Italian doctor and epidemiologist who writes simply and truthfully about nutrition and therapeutic practices like fasting in "LaGrande Via," an association, a book and website. As readers, we would like to take this opportunity to thank him for the work he has done over the years.

3

Social Interaction

Have you ever wondered how many people pass through your life every day (and vice versa)? Have you ever made note of how many of them you've actually exchanged words with?

Have you ever thought about how you came into contact with these people (and vice versa)? You have come to know *us*, your authors, a bit better by now, as we start the third chapter. Sometimes the thoughts we share might seem a bit lazy, but they give us inspiration for our practical life. These are valid thoughts for a book, but also for understanding us better as human beings and becoming better people.

For math lovers, we are sorry to say that, after careful analysis, we don't believe we can assign numeric values to these interactions. We realized that the place where you live, the work that you do, and your lifestyle all significantly influence the number of people you encounter throughout your day. We also realized that some days we don't see or speak to anyone, whereas other days one look over dinner tells us that we spoke to far too many people that day and we need a break—so we enjoy our dinner in silence.

Beyond numbers, this does not mean that these encounters don't considerably influence our lives and those of others. Yes, you read that right, even those of others. This chapter introduces the idea that our rituals of gratitude can also have a direct impact on the lives of others.

Let's approach this in an orderly fashion. In the fourth century BC, in his book *Politics*, Aristotle wrote that man is by nature a social animal. We often accept this truth without question. But what does "social animal" mean, exactly? What types of relationships make us different from other animals? Do we really form relationships solely for assistance and defense, as Darwin theorized? We believe there's much more to it than that, so we have dedicated the next seven rituals to moments in which we interact with others because we think they deserve greater awareness.

Since this subject of relationships is very broad, we have decided to address it very gently. Therefore, we don't talk about husbands and wives, children, live-in partners, or mothers and fathers (which are addressed in another chapter), but rather casual, often fleeting encounters that we have on the street, in a store or bar, at the post office, or on public transportation. These encounters last just a few seconds. They could be with the person who delivers a package you ordered online, someone who stops you on the street for directions, or the person behind you in the supermarket line who only needs to pay for a carton of milk while your cart is full. The moments in which our kindness and gratitude can directly influence our lives and those of others are numerous. In addition, in many of these situations we might find ourselves on the other side; and, in that case, we can decide how to act and what ritual to apply.

As you read the next few pages, you might find yourself saying "I always do this. My grandma taught me!" We are glad that the teachings of grandmothers persist and that some people do them without thinking. You should, therefore, focus more on celebrating these moments, bestowing them with the right importance, and thanking your grandma for having passed along the good habit as well as the person before you for having given you the possibility to be an active part of this moment of healthy interaction. The more we are able to value these little moments, the more our lives and those of people receiving this attention will raise the positive energy in the world.

Others might instead be discovering these practices for the first time. They come from traditions that suggested approaching others with a sort of respectful reverence thousands of years ago. We are also glad to be a part of this revelation, and we hope that you are curious to see the results of experiencing these practices.

Lastly, some of the rituals we pulled out from the depths of our bookshelves might sound new and maybe a bit strange. "Do I really have a superpower? Can I really become the James Bond of happiness? Are you sure?" Like always, we invite you to test them out for yourselves! Introduce one ritual a day, paying attention to what changes inside and, more importantly, outside of you. The true value of these little actions is in transforming our lives and those of others in simple ways. If you are able to do so without too many expectations, you will find that you are making this wonderful planet a better place for everyone without even realizing it.

Good Manners Are Always in Style

01

FEDERICA — When I was a girl, my mother would tell me to greet people and thank them when they did something for me. And I was happy to oblige, because these people would always respond openly and politely. Without knowing it, my mother was confirming the theory of the famous clinical psychologist Jordan B. Peterson. In his book *12 Rules for Life*, he invites parents to assume responsibility for educating their children in order to make the community a more pleasant place, which will then welcome them more appropriately when they become adults. Receiving a polite response from someone you have greeted or thanked is always nice. Imagine entering a cafe, ordering a coffee, drinking it, and leaving immediately without greeting the person who made your coffee, thanking them for it, or saying good-bye when you left. What kind of person would this make you?! Many people have forgotten the basics of good manners, first and foremost greeting and thanking, but also giving up your seat to an elderly person on the subway, helping a mother get her stroller on the bus, or holding the door open for the next person entering or leaving. It's not only a matter of manners, but also a way to honor the people you encounter, look at them with your heart, and know that they exist just like us. When we ignore others and remain immersed in our own thoughts, our energy also invites others to ignore us.

Yoga, the discipline I have the honor of teaching, expresses this idea with its traditional greeting "Namaste," which means "The divine light in me bows to the divine light within you." Is it not beautiful to greet others with sincere gratitude for shared moments when our lives cross each other's, even when the other person is a stranger?

In Another's Shoes

02

SIMONE — Plato was so cool. He was Socrates' student and Aristotle's teacher, and all three together were like the Avengers of ancient Greek philosophy. It would be like playing soccer with Pelé and then becoming Ronaldo's coach (the Brazilian, not the Portuguese one). I'm very fond of Plato, especially because of a saying that is said to be attributed to him: "Be kind, for everyone you meet is fighting a hard battle."

Paying attention to the battles others are fighting is very difficult for me. It's like the saying "Put yourself in another's shoes." But every time I try to imagine myself in the shoes of someone else, I am hit with a great sense of discomfort. How am I supposed to know what another person is living? Did they have a terrible day and the world came crashing down on them? Or are they just a selfish and demanding person who wants to take advantage of other people's kindness for their own motives? These thoughts that cross my mind in a fraction of a second often paralyze me and lead me to inaction. When I come to, the first words that come to mind are those of Pope Francis: "Who am I to judge?" Francesco, you are absolutely right. Thank you for being a continuous source of inspiration. But how might I remember this a second earlier rather than later, when it's often too late?

In our research, we have encountered a sort of magical potion that any wise person has in some way or another distilled in their own terms: act with kindness. Kindness is truly a cure-all for diffusing tension. The next time that you are unsure how to react to someone, imagine yourself in their shoes and give them a big smile. The benefits of this magic potion will surprise you.

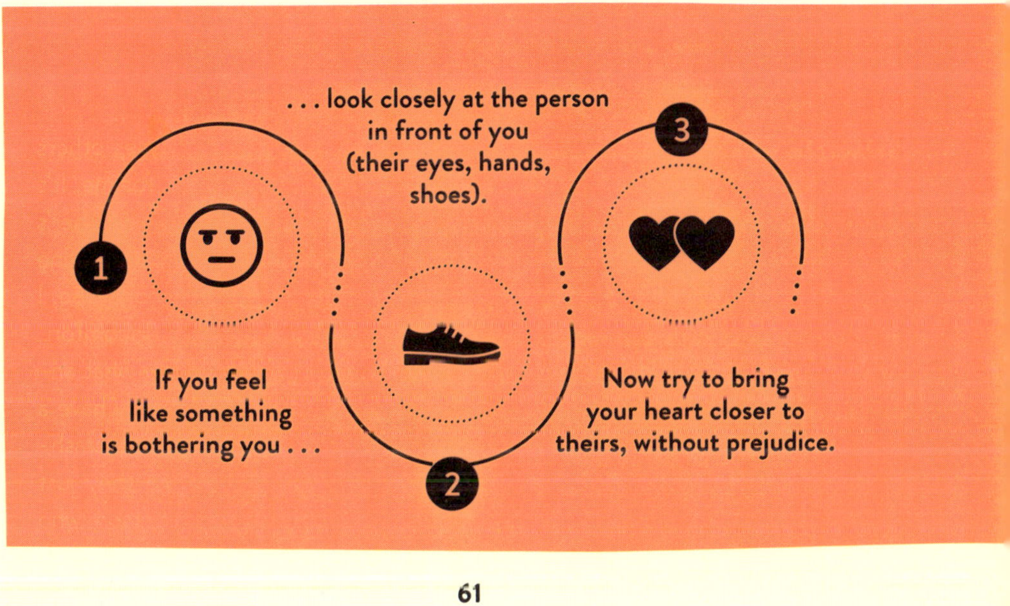

The Other Line Is Always Faster

03

SIMONE — If you haven't yet seen *The Brand New Testament*, you must watch it! It tells the story of a cynical god who created the world so that he could relax and stay busy, but then he got carried away with tormenting the lives of human beings. His power is diminished when his daughter hacks his computer and tells every person on earth when they will die. Knowing exactly how much time they have left, the people feel freed of their chains and begin doing what they've always dreamed of. The film offers a series of funny but profound thoughts. In this chapter, I would like to borrow from Law 2128 in the film: "The other line is always moving faster."

Lines, people, and situations that don't move as fast as we would like often make us nervous, moody, and unpleasant. But there is a remedy for these situations as well. No, it's not a people-evaporating gun. It's something we all possess but when unused goes to waste: Patience.

The proverb "Patience is a virtue" is a valuable lesson, but how might we apply it when we are standing in line at the supermarket or sitting in traffic on the highway? This ritual is once again borrowed from Vietnamese Buddhism, and it is carried out in two steps. The first is—again—called Awareness. Are we really late, or did we just not expect this traffic? What's really bothering us? It's a chance to investigate where that frustration is coming from. Since you have nothing else to do, you might as well listen to yourself.

The second step is Acceptance. Can we do anything about it? Accepting that we don't have full control over what happens in the world is the fruit of great humility as well as common sense. Using these two actions together will not only allow us to reduce stress but also understand that delays and lines can become a blessing, and for this we must give thanks.

Time for Others Brings Abundance

04

FEDERICA — Some time ago I was invited to participate in a meditation series with Deepak Chopra on abundance. It helped me realize that one of the greatest errors we make in life is not fully understanding the meaning of the words we use. The first task Chopra assigned was to define what the word "abundance" encompasses. Let's stop here. Get a piece of paper and pen and try to describe what abundance means to you. If you approach it as I did the first time, you will find yourselves with a lot of references to material things. In those days of meditation, I pushed myself beyond the limits of my vocabulary and discovered that the meaning of the word "abundance" was full of possibilities, people, knowledge, talent, and opportunities; and material elements weren't present.

The people we meet randomly every day can be a source of inspiration and intuition, whether it's from a random encounter or an unexpected invitation. Deeper relationships can arise from anywhere.

Another very important experience related to this was when I took part in a meeting—in the library of the mountain town where we spend the summer—with the organization "The Human Library," a project founded by Ronni Abergel in Copenhagen in 2000. It uses people as personified books (the book of one's life) to respond to questions that others might have as "readers." These questions are often things that wouldn't normally be addressed in conversations between strangers.

Sitting next to a stranger, giving them your time, and sharing the intimacy of a casual interaction was a wonderful experience, and I know that it allowed us to enrich each other's lives. It would be great to have many "Human Libraries" throughout the world. We suggest "wasting" time with others, especially if you don't know who they are. Trust your instinct, and at the end of your interaction you will be thanking each other.

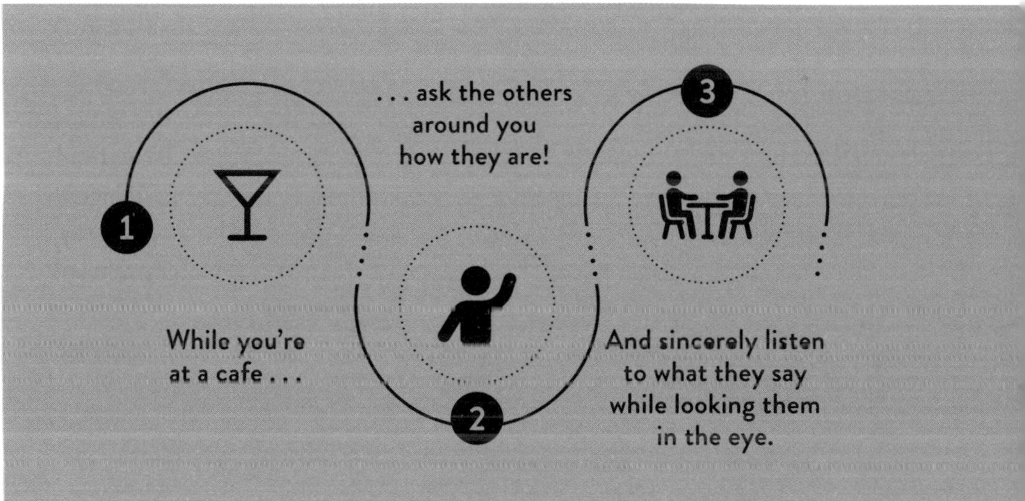

The Superpower You Didn't Know You Had

05

FEDERICA — The world is made of energy! When I say this, the people around me often smile. However, it wasn't me who had this genius revelation! It was Albert Einstein who said "Everything is energy, and that's all there is to it." Einstein was a physicist but never lazed under apple trees. Einstein believed first and foremost that everything is made of energy, including us. Energy is expressed through frequencies and vibrations, and we know this even though we pretend to ignore it. Think about when you enter a meeting and think, "Wow, the air is tense in here. . . ." Or when you return home and know immediately that your partner had a difficult day, so you go to hug them to relieve their stress.

The ritual we suggest here has two phases. The first is that you have to tune in to the frequency of the environment you are entering in order to quickly process the information your senses are picking up on. Record the situation and then decide what to do. You can align yourself, for good or for bad, to the energy that's already circulating, or you can use your superpower to flood the space and people with positive, crystal-clear energy.

Use your breath and your deep awareness to generate positive vibes and try to channel calm and serenity. I often try to use it in places where the combination of people and the unknown environment makes me uncomfortable because I can sense the confused intentions. Like a DJ, I start playing with the levels of my emotions and energy, focusing on positive, calm thoughts aimed at the people around me.

Give thanks for this superpower that already resides within you. You only have to find it and put it to use.

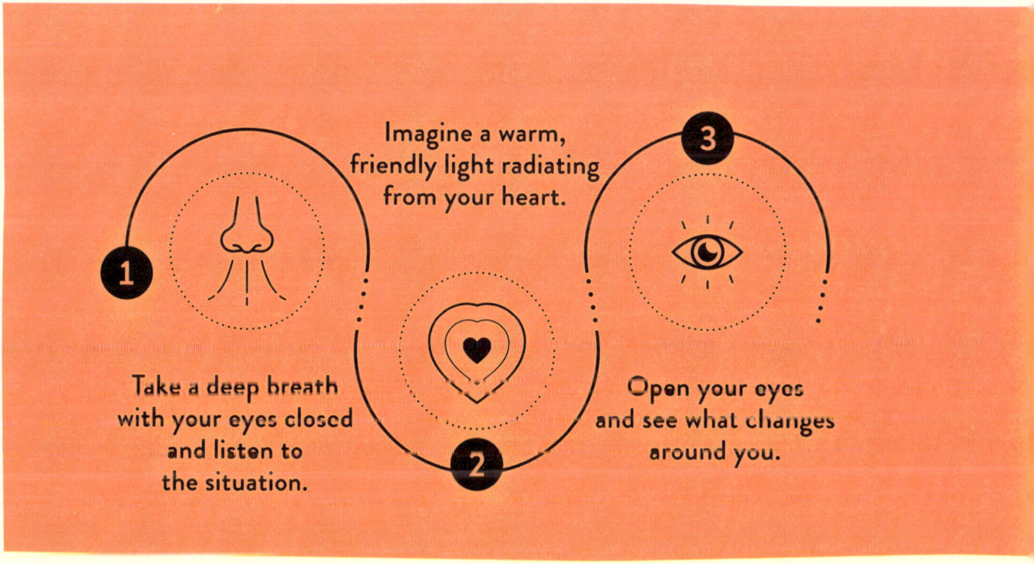

Respect! (Feat. A. Franklin)

06

SIMONE — Aretha Franklin had an incredible voice. We should thank artists like her every day for blessing us with the sounds, words, and emotions that fill our lives.

This song in particular has an important message. "All I'm askin' is for a little respect when you come home." Federica always laughs that our home tasks are well defined. She likes cooking, and I find washing dishes super relaxing. Her mother is still surprised to see her daughter sitting relaxed after lunch, because tidying up and washing dishes is my job. The division of tasks in our house is so clear that we don't even need to talk about it. We accept our differences and use them to our advantage. I am convinced that having a role means you also carry certain responsibilities. Believing you can do everything comes from an obtuse perspective, whereas accepting the space in which your talents are most appropriate is a sign of humility and awareness.

How many times a day do you want to do something you don't know how to do and, more importantly, for which you don't want to bear the responsibility? You might believe you're quicker than the kid working at the nearby fruit stand and that it would have taken you less time to do what he does. Is that really the case? Consider also what your colleague did this morning, your child at school, or the person in front of you. How many things do you actually want to do? How many people are you trying to be?

Try to wake the memory of what you know and what you want to do, and when you do it, do so as well as you can and with the best intentions. Leave space for others. Respect differences. Help others express themselves in the way they know how instead of judging them. Do you promise you'll do so tomorrow with the reception attendant? Then give thanks for their talents and show them a smile as you hum *Respect*!

The Secret Agents of Happiness

07

SIMONE — Federica loves surprises. Although every time I say "I have a surprise for you," she responds "Is it a puppy?" It's clearly a subliminal message I pretend not to hear. I'm always happy when I'm able to surprise her, because it has taught me that it doesn't take much (a bag of roasted chestnuts, a bar of chocolate, etc.) to make someone's day special. And in this vein of thought, I would like to propose the final ritual of this chapter, which is the most exciting one to us. The ritual is to give someone a little gift without expecting thanks in return because . . . they don't know who we are! And now you might be asking, how do I do that? It's simple. Look closely and be clever. In Italy, there is a tradition called "caffè sospeso," which is when you drink a coffee but pay for two, leaving one for someone who comes after you. This is just one idea. You can do the same when you buy food. The cashier will know when to give your gift to someone who really needs it. Do you live in an apartment building? Maybe consider volunteering to distribute mail to the various tenants. Sometimes, when we make a cake or big lunch, we'll take some leftovers to the homeless person in our neighborhood.

Our model is Charles "Chuck" Feeney, the Irish-American founder of Duty Free Shoppers Group. He was one of the richest people in the world for a few years with his more than 7-billion-dollar empire. More than 40 years ago, he began donating his estate without anyone realizing it, supporting his philanthropic foundation literally in secret. Donating everything we have could be an arduous task, so let's start with little gifts. We will soon feel a personal sense of gratitude growing inside us.

Notes and Sources

01 GOOD MANNERS ARE ALWAYS IN STYLE. "Namaste" is the most beautiful greeting. *Namas*, meaning "I bow," and *te*, meaning "to you," add spiritual significance to your greetings and blessing of the divine qualities present in others.

---

02 IN ANOTHER'S SHOES. In his book *The Name of God Is Mercy,* Pope Francis talks about "sclerocardia," which means "the hardening of a judging heart." We too hope that everyone can rediscover that their heart is made of flesh and blood, not stone.

---

03 THE OTHER LINE IS ALWAYS FASTER. If you haven't seen it, watch *The Brand New Testament*. In addition to what we've already discussed, the theme of the film is very useful. If we knew how much time we had left, what would we do with it?

---

04 TIME FOR OTHERS BRINGS ABUNDANCE. The Human Library is an important project that you can find at the link humanlibrary.org. We think the name is wonderful, for starters, because after all, if you look closer, that's exactly what we are, each a beautiful book. It's magical to find time and ways to open yourself up and truly listen to others.

---

05 THE SUPERPOWER YOU DIDN'T KNOW YOU HAD. Let's be honest: quantum physics is not a subject for the dinner table. However, in his books *The Order of Time* and *Reality Is Not What It Seems*, Italian physicist Carlo Rovelli fluidly explains what energy is as well as the concepts of space, time, and matter.

---

06 RESPECT! (FEAT. A. FRANKLIN). *Yin* and *yang*, positive and negative, male and female. Balance is a precarious game and something we must always keep in mind. *Yin Yang: La Dynamique du Monde* by Cyrille J.-D. Javary is another book we recommend if you want to further study the dynamic matter of things and better understand why balance is so hard to maintain but an objective we must pursue.

---

07 THE SECRET AGENTS OF HAPPINESS. To find out more about the work of Charles "Chuck" Feeney, go to AtlanticPhilanthropies.org and look through the projects he has supported around the world. In September 2020, Chuck officially achieved his goal of giving away all his money to charity and subsequently closed his foundation.

4 Family & Friends

Now that we've explored rituals surrounding relationships with strangers in chapter 3, are we ready to level up, like in an old videogame? This chapter also addresses relationships but focuses on the deeper daily ones we have with family and friends. In these relationships, rituals of gratitude can be expressed to their maximum potential.

Why? Because, as we said at the beginning of the book, an action becomes a ritual when it is repeated over a certain period of time. Considering that we spend a lot of time, do many things, and "a lot happens" with the people we are discussing in this chapter, it's the perfect opportunity to create new habits.

First, let's identify more specifically who we would include in this category of people. To simplify, we tend to divide them into two big groups: those we chose and those we . . . didn't choose directly. We say "not directly" because many of you probably know and embrace the theory that Einstein masterfully expressed as "God does not play dice with the universe." In other words, nothing is random. If we take this as our unquestionable starting point, then even our parents, our siblings, and our family as a whole are not the product of a gamble of fate. We know this might seem like a simplistic argument, but think about it before you shake your head and say "You make it sound simple, but this model doesn't apply to my situation!" In this chapter, we have added a new rule: For the following actions, you cannot use this as an excuse, sorry!

But let's get back to family, our extended circle, including childhood friends, "aunts" and "uncles," your babysitter who you always called aunt (no . . . not mommy), colleagues who are more friends than colleagues, family friends we spent memorable vacations with, and so on.

Rituals have been important within family life since the time of hunter-gatherers. Think about when a tribe had to scavenge for food at the end of summer and would come across a tree with mature fruit. It would become a moment of collective feasting that guaranteed everyone had the calories they needed for the week ahead. Or think about Thanksgiving today, in which millions of American families come together, no matter what, to give thanks to god for the harvest and what they received throughout the year. Similarly, there's Christmas and Eid al-Fitr, the end of the Muslim holiday of Ramadan. These are collective rituals that are fundamental for human beings and communities around the globe.

In this chapter, we discuss moments that we all know well. The list is long, and each of us has our own (Sunday lunch, phone calls at the end of the day, New Year's at the neighbors', etc.), but the important thing is that we ask you to do something a bit different than usual. We would like you to take a small step back before potentially taking two steps forward.

The step back we would like you to take starts with these rituals, which are already an integral part of your lives, and it involves being just a little more aware as you do them. You won't have to change anything in your weekly trip to visit grandma at the nursing home or your aunt who lives alone. We just ask that you pause to think about what's happening inside of you as you take the same road you always do. What deep feelings emerge within you? Compassion? Boredom? Affection? Indifference? Can you not wait to get back in the car and go home, or are you grateful that your grandma remembered the first time you jumped in the river near your house? We feel the need to say that this feeling—whether it's positive, negative, or neutral—is very important and should be brought to your attention, valued. It is the first step in initiating a process of deep transformation toward members of your family. Often we find ourselves living automatically, without examining what happens within us and thus without endowing our actions with the right value.

In this chapter, we wanted to dedicate a ritual to our friends and relatives who have passed away as well. In some parts of the world, including our own, death is a difficult subject, but we believe it is a very important moment for families, and it should be valued and celebrated as much as life is.

We'll say it again: the best way to verify how effective these actions are is to try them yourself, even if you believe you'll never manage to be patient with your brother. In any case, for a few minutes a day, try to give credit to the masters of thousand-year-old traditions who have devoted their lives to making ours better.

Never Go Empty-Handed

01

SIMONE — Have you ever heard the expression "You're invited to dinner only if you knock with your feet?" I heard it for the first time recently, and I admit that I had to ask for an explanation. My guest slyly suggested that I try visiting him with so many gifts in my arms that it was impossible to knock with anything but my feet.

Smiling, I remembered years ago when, in India, I often found myself knocking with my feet as I traveled from one Tibetan monastery to the next. Tibetans have a long tradition of hospitality, and I never showed up at someone's house without something to celebrate our gathering. If we think about it, bringing a present is a nice way to enter someone's house. It is a small celebration, as well as a sign of respect. The beautiful thing about Tibetans is that the value of the gift is not important. No one expects anything of value. It's the gesture that matters. For my first meeting with the 17th Karmapa, Trinley Thaye Dorje, I made this Tibetan spirit my own and brought a huge bag of potato chips! I smile thinking about the young Simone, but I probably wouldn't do the same today. However, my spirit back then was genuine, and I am sure that the Karmapa could feel it—maybe even smiled too, deep down.

I am sure that none of you goes to dinner at a friend's house without a bottle of wine or tub of ice cream, but I invite you to extend this habit to less formal situations as well. For example, when you return from work and your partner is waiting at home. Bringing a piece of chocolate or a container of raspberries or strawberries home is proof that during the day, there was a moment in which your thoughts about that person became concrete action.

Without even realizing it, you set in motion beneficial energy that comes from your thoughts and will remain in the air until all the raspberries are finished, or even longer. It is almost a perpetual engine of gratitude that the world is in desperate need of!

The Theater of Mistakes

02

FEDERICA — "The apple doesn't fall far from the tree," my psychotherapist and analyst told me in one of our first sessions. The first thing I thought was "Great! She also loves common expressions. We'll get along well!" I didn't know that this would be the beginning of a difficult journey that I still carry with immense gratitude in my heart to this day. At that time, I discovered wonderful things about myself: for example, that I am not immortal, that I wouldn't be young forever, and that I continued to repeat certain behavioral patterns. And I also learned that family is a network of relationships that we are part of, whether we want to be or not.

Years later, during a yoga lesson, someone told me about the theory of family and systemic constellations, and the subject interested me so much that I decided to look into it more. That was how I had one of the strangest and most revealing experiences of my life. Without going into the details, I would like to share how Bert Hellinger's therapeutic method opened my mind. Within a family, each of us is a character we play so well that we are not able to truly connect with others. The Russian theater director Konstantin Stanislavski developed an acting method that asked actors to identify with their characters in order to "feel them," a sort of physiology of emotions that could activate the "magic if," that part of us that is able to enter an experience, even if we've never lived it.

So, what does this all have to do with feeling gratitude toward our families? We often think about family relationships in a way that puts us at the center. I deserve, I expect, I did. . . .

Well, then, for one week, try to identify with another person within your family unit, whoever you want. It is a strong and disturbing experience; but if you try, you will be grateful that you experienced the performance and mistakes of another with your heart.

Do You Remember?

03

FEDERICA — Recently, I had to tidy my childhood bedroom at my parents' house for some maintenance work. I started out thinking I would find it very boring, but actually the afternoon I spent there was fun and sentimental. Left abandoned in drawers among old planners were photos and postcards—from the 1980s, when we would send postcards to friends and family while traveling—and I started to take photos of everything before cleaning. Then I sent the photos to friends, asking them "Do you remember?" Retracing the years of my life opened up a world of memories, some happy, others less so.

I think the art of remembering is so important, something we've lost today. I'm not the only one to say so. Numerous studies also agree. We live in an age in which the "overloading" of social media and the digital world is almost drowning our brains. Therefore, we need to once again reactivate the parts of our brains we use for memory. In addition, sharing memories with friends and family is a beautiful ritual that helps reinforce our relationships. Remembering with others the class trips, vacations, special and happy moments, or difficult ones we had to overcome helps us strengthen relationships with the people that belong to such a close and important circle. Don't make comparisons. Don't look at whether your family is small or if you can count your friends on one hand. Size (when we talk about loved ones) is not important at all. You can make a difference and inject strong emotional energy into your relationships by simply using the words "Do you remember?" It's a sort of affectionate glue. It will be interesting and beautiful to notice how those moments will bring you back to the little details you might have forgotten. You'll reexperience the successes you've achieved over time. Use these memories to be grateful for the time that has passed.

9999, 9998, 9997 . . .

04

FEDERICA — There are times when gatherings with friends and family become Greek tragedies. Quite often this happens because we already wrote the script, assigning each person their part; and therefore, we are ready for when others do . . . exactly what we expect of them! Someone will talk about politics, someone else will criticize your friend's vegan diet, someone will ask about your romantic life, which you think is going well but your grandma thinks is a big disaster. Staying calm in these moments is difficult but important.

Luckily, there's an ancient and infallible technique that can help us when we are close to our boiling point. It's called Pranayama, or breath control. It's often associated with yoga because Patanjali, the author of *Yoga Sutra*, includes it as the fourth of the fundamental points of that method. However, Pranayama can also be practiced independently of asanas. Translated from Sanskrit, it means "the ability to control and expand the flow of vital energy through techniques like breathing and meditation." In the Notes, you can find information to learn more about it. But here you will find a simple exercise for the next time you have lunch with your family.

Remember the famous saying "Count to ten before you speak?" Well, all you have to do is add breathing to this concept. When you feel like you are reaching a difficult moment, start focusing only on your breath, listen to it, and try to understand if you are using only the upper part of your chest. Good, then stare at a fixed point and count to five as you inhale through your nose, pause for three seconds, and exhale for another five. Repeat this five times without losing count. No one will notice, and you will thank your body and lungs for helping you return to a state of calm that makes the conversation more manageable. Try it! 9999, 9998, 9997. . . .

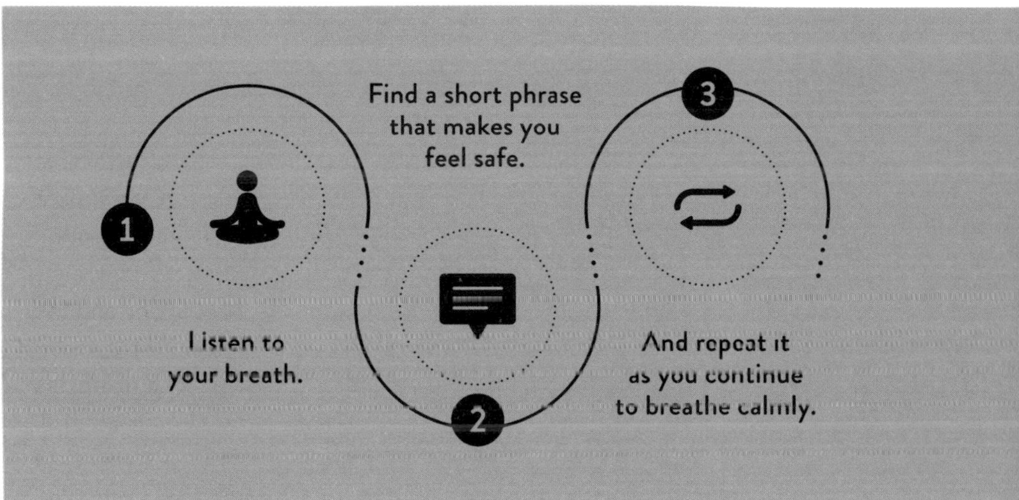

Karmageddon

05

SIMONE — The expression "Karmageddon" entered my vocabulary after seeing the film *A Shaun the Sheep Movie: Farmageddon*. I found the comparison between Armageddon, the final battle between good and evil described in the Apocalypse, with Shaun's farm and his clay friends genius, and it immediately inspired me. Today, "karma" is used in common language, but not everyone knows its true meaning. The term comes from the Sanskrit and can be translated as "action" or "doing, obtaining, completing."

Therefore, karma can be considered something that is created through action. Of course, comparing our actions to the battle of all battles might seem a bit of a stretch, but I'm sure you'll agree that sometimes conflict—metaphorical or otherwise—with our family is comparable to that described in the Gospel of John. But what can we do in everyday life to manage these battles? How can we establish habits that can muffle the tone of these often conflictual relationships? Since we are talking about karma, we should refer directly to the words of the historic Buddha, who affirmed in *Anguttara Nikaya* that actions guided by intention (*cetana* in Sanskrit) always produce consequences. In practice, Buddha reminds us that every thought we have, every action we take, every word we say, always depends on our choices, and these choices have effects.

So, what is the intention the Buddha is talking about? It is the fulcrum of our ritual. Before doing, saying, or thinking something, pay careful attention to why you are doing, saying, or thinking it.

Stop a second before, listen closely, and search for what is moving within you. These often are emotions that don't have anything to do with what we are talking about. So why not renounce an unnecessary battle from the start? You will be giving yourself and your family a true gift!

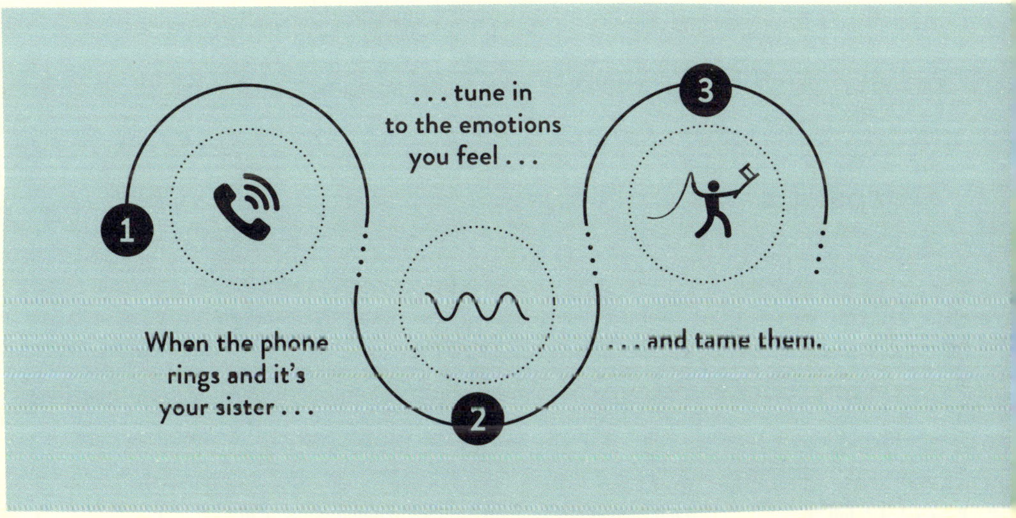

"06"

The Day of the Dead

FEDERICA — I love Pixar films and find their plots genius. They are able to address difficult topics with a levity that moves me, and I've found myself crying next to children in the cinema more than once. One of the animated films I love most is *Coco*. Forgive me, I'm terrible at writing summaries, but it's essentially the story of a boy, Miguel, and his dog, Dante, who go on a journey to the land of the dead. The film is based on Mexican traditions, and it struck me how naturally some cultures are able to intertwine the two worlds, the visible and the invisible. Miguel's journey inspired my relationship with people who are no longer with us. There are moments when we need to confront the death of someone we loved who shared their time with us. This ritual is for them: a brief moment every day in which we think about the people who have passed on, those whose names and faces we remember and those who came at the beginning of our family's origins, all those people, mother after mother, child after child, who led to us, here and now. It is thanks to them that we are here reading this book. And we exist not only because of life but also because of death.

Every day, acknowledge and thank your grandparents, parents, siblings, aunts and uncles, and friends who have passed away. If you can pass along this tradition to your children, they will do so with theirs as well and so on, creating an everlasting energy that will sustain the memory of your family.

Look At the Bright Side

07

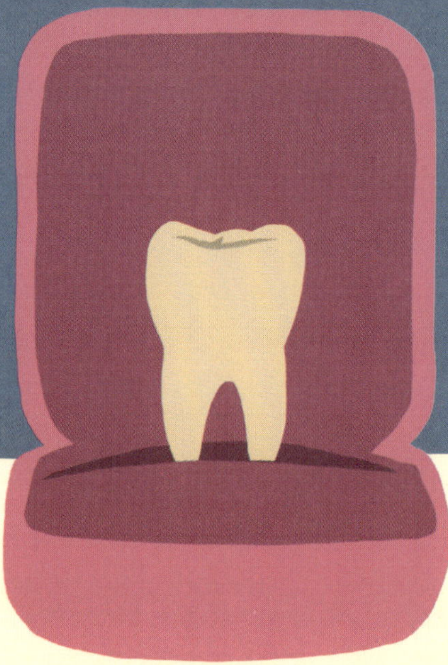

SIMONE — The title of this chapter seems like a simple play on words, but it contains a truth that many masters have told, using metaphors and parables. In choosing how to share this simple but very powerful ritual, I decided to turn to Rudolf Steiner. Many of you probably know him for his teaching methods that led to his schools, but Steiner has a vast and heterogeneous set of work. He is the founder of Anthroposophy and crosses many disciplines, from agriculture to architecture, addressing subject matter that appears contrasting, like karma and Jesus Christ. Even if we don't all believe in his philosophy, I think Steiner is someone worth knowing, to see what effect he might have on you. If you want to explore his vision of the world, try reading *The Philosophy of Freedom*.

This ritual draws inspiration from

the fourth of his five exercises of freedom: positivity. This consists of constantly searching for goodness, beauty, and excellence in all people, things, and experiences. This concept is found in an ancient Persian legend about Jesus Christ, who, as he walks with his disciples, sees the decaying corpse of a dog on the side of the road. His disciples look away from the horrific scene, whereas Christ stops, looks at the dog thoughtfully, and says "What beautiful teeth this creature had!" This is the spirit of our ritual. Look for beauty in the people around you, especially those you spend and have spent time with. If you look, you will always find something; and when you find it, don't be shy. Thank this relative or friend with your heart for the good you've seen in them—even if it's just a nice set of teeth!

Notes and Sources

01 NEVER GO EMPTY-HANDED. Generosity is one of the greatest virtues we can adopt; it is an intense act of kindness. We suggest looking for more information about Metta meditation, or the meditation of kindness, which tries to awaken our pure and neutral love.

---

02 THE THEATER OF MISTAKES. To find out more about family constellations, you can read the book *Metagenealogy* by Alejandro Jodorowsky and Marianne Costa. You will discover that family is the place where the subconsciouses of all its members interact.

---

03 DO YOU REMEMBER? If you struggle to remember things and events, try understanding why. Memory is a muscle that must be exercised. In *Moonwalking with Einstein: The Art and Science of Remembering Everything*, author Joshua Foer demonstrates that memory is a gift we all have, but we often ignore its potential.

---

04 9999, 9998, 9997. . . Pranayama consists of different techniques. To dip your toes in the subject matter, you can read *Pranayama: The Energetics of Breath* by André Van Lysebeth. It is a fundamental text by one of today's yoga masters.

---

05 **KARMAGEDDON.** Excellent guides on the interconnections between actions and people are the podcasts by Marco Ferrini, founder of the Center for Bhaktivedanta Studies, and by Deepak Chopra. We are never alone in our actions, whether we are with family or not. Remember the famous butterfly that flapped its wings and caused a hurricane on the other side of the world?

06 **THE DAY OF THE DEAD.** In addition to the film *Coco*, we also recommend Ricky Gervais's *After Life*. Gervais would probably find it strange to be cited in a book on gratitude and kindness, but we like him because his cynicism hides the depth of his soul, something that perhaps not even he would admit to having.

07 **LOOK AT THE BRIGHT SIDE.** *The Wise Heart* by Jack Kornfield is a book you should always have on your nightstand. If you don't have it, go now! It's nice to flip through now and then. One of the first chapters is dedicated to searching for nobility and beauty in all human beings. This is a quality that we struggle to find first and foremost in ourselves, let alone in others, according to psychoanalyst Robert A. Johnson.

5 Me Time

We talk about wanting to find time for ourselves, yet we struggle to do so.

We would like to start this chapter by trying to make sense of what that means. What exactly do we think about when we want time for ourselves? What expectations do we have? What makes these moments valuable opportunities for our spirit?

When we talk about time for ourselves, one of the first thoughts that often comes to mind is doing physical activity. This is probably because it makes us think of ways to connect our body and mind, something that allows us to feel present, united, connected, to bring these two parts of ourselves together so that we don't necessarily live them separately.

At other times, however, we might instinctively think of time for ourselves as reading a book, going to see an exhibition, focusing on a hobby, seeing a film, or taking a trip to somewhere special and evocative. If these are the activities that help restore you and find your center, then we believe that's the best option for you. However, we decided to make these seven rituals a little different and to connect them to opportunities in which we use our senses to listen to and get to know ourselves better, thus allowing us to appreciate the amazing organism that is our body as more than just a physical object every day.

For this, we have drawn inspiration from Ayurveda, a discipline that places much importance on the fact that we are what we are because of our senses, which receive stimuli and help us explore the world. We want to restore the importance of listening to our senses by suggesting daily moments in which you can appreciate them through actions that help you understand their fundamental role.

By now, we know how important it is to pay attention when things are spoken in whispers, forcing us to lean in to hear what's being said. Therefore, time for ourselves in this chapter is an explosion of sensorial gratitude, for our skin, our eyes, and our ears!

The wellness industry reminds us that moving and taking care of ourselves is advantageous. We want to add a bit of sweetness to this. When it comes to personal wellbeing, we are too often overwhelmed by forward-moving energy, a feeling of constant struggle. The important thing, however, is to allow your sensations to take control.

According to recent studies, global investment in physical activity has doubled. Whether you are weight-lifting in a gym, finding time to play soccer with your children, or jogging, you know that moving gratifies the body and mind. We know from experience that movement is beneficial to our nervous system. Many important neurotransmitters serve our wellbeing. Oxytocin, for example, promotes self-confidence and often is considered the neurotransmitter of love. Serotonin, also called the happiness hormone, regulates sleep, mood, and appetite.

The rituals we recommend, like massages, repeating mantras, listening to silence, and developing your sense of smell will help your body develop a series of neurological habits that are as beneficial as the physical activity already mentioned. Our objective is obviously not to substitute movement, but rather to integrate the movement you already do with other actions that can increase your sense of daily wellbeing and help you look at your body with immense gratitude, for its shape and size and ability to make you feel good!

Receptive Receptors

01

FEDERICA — I have often relived moments in my life through the scent of something specific, like an iris, which reminds me of the perfume my beloved Aunt Tata wore, or lavender, which I've always used when I sleep. Olfactory memory allows us to remember a smell and associate it with a physical or emotional memory, meaning it can later bring back the memory. Through it, we can clearly revisit an old experience, even those buried deep in our minds. Our sense of smell is perhaps the most enigmatic of the senses but is also the most powerful for our subconscious. It resists time. Marcel Proust spoke about it when he found himself remembering his childhood after simply trying a *madeleine* (which he wrote about in his masterpiece *In Search of Lost Time*). The limbic system is the area of the brain that operates the sense of smell, and it is directly connected to emotions (amygdala) and memory (hippocampus). This explains why memories that emerge through smells are vivid and immediate.

A study by the Department of Neurogenetics and Behavior at Rockefeller University in New York published in *Nature* shows that people can remember 35 percent of the things they smell, compared to only 5 percent of what they see, 2 percent of what they hear, and 1 percent of what they touch. In addition, they discovered that humans can recognize a trillion smells. Therefore, if you have mistreated your nose, it's time to take care of it. Look for smells that can give you energy in the morning (orange, lemon, and eucalyptus), help you relax (lavender, Roman chamomile, and sweet orange), alleviate headaches (spearmint, basil, and rose), and help with concentration (bergamot, lemongrass, and verbena). You will thank these wonderful plants for saving you!

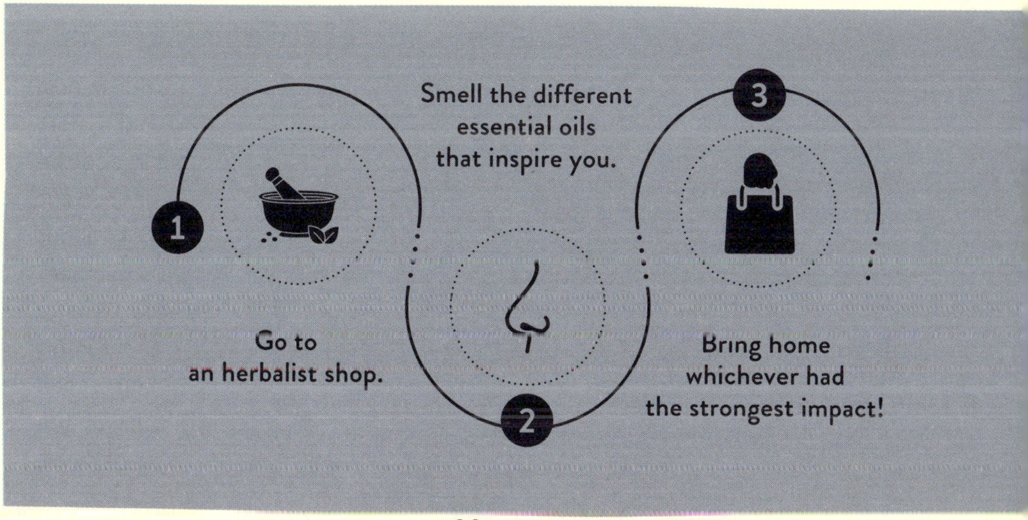

An Ocean of Sensations

02

FEDERICA — I am a huge fan of cultures with wellbeing rituals for the body. Perhaps this is because one of my favorite places on earth is Finland! I still remember feeling like a queen when I found the sauna in my rented house on the first vacation I spent there! In Finland, saunas are an integral part of the culture. It's not a way to treat yourself, but rather a priority. It's estimated that there is one sauna for every two people in Finland. It is so rooted in the culture that there is even a legend about it. The Saunatonttu gnome is the spirit of the sauna that punishes anyone who misbehaves in saunas. This gnome must be honored by always keeping the fire lit.

Like saunas, ancient Roman baths, Turkish *hammams*, Russian *banyas*, Native American sweat lodges, Japanese *onsens*, and Mexican *temazcals* are all useful ways to reclaim your body and skin through steam and hot water. These moments can also include rubbing your skin with a horsehair brush or willow or beech branches.

Our skin is the largest sensory organ, but we often ignore it, only thinking of it in terms of hygiene. But because it offers us so much, our skin needs to be treated and loved. In the absence of a sauna or other particular treatments, one of my secrets requires only a bathtub. Fill the bathtub with hot water and dissolve half a kilo of salt, then add dried seaweed (kelp is the best) and a natural sponge. Find a playlist with the sound of waves (there are many) and immerse yourself in the water, scrubbing your skin every so often with the sponge. You have just recreated your own little sea, which benefits your skin, liver, and thyroid.

You can also try dry-brushing to stimulate circulation and the lymphatic system. This is called *garshana* in Ayurveda. Or you can give yourself a massage with warm sesame oil. In any case, take care of yourself and treat this organ with gratitude and generosity!

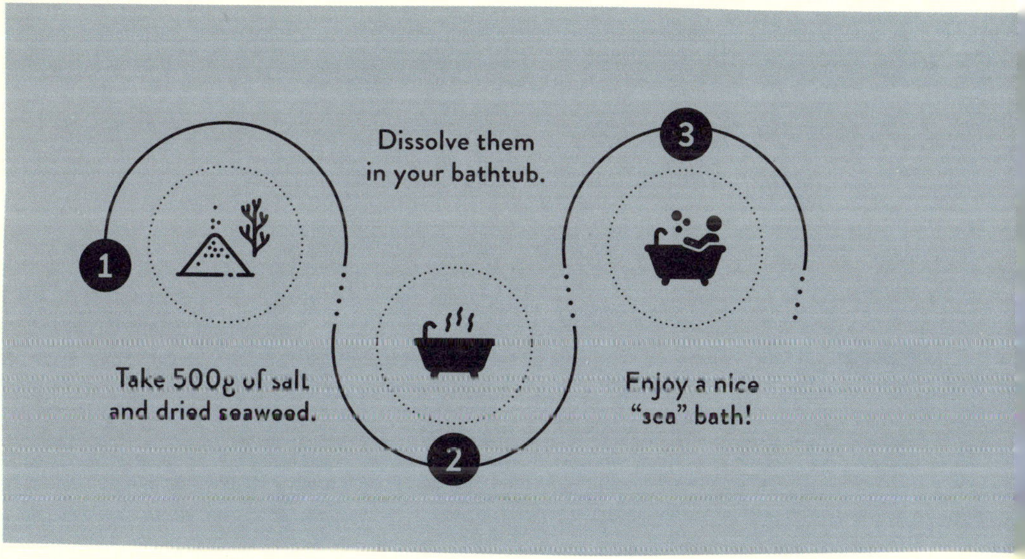

The Sound That Vibrates Within Us

03

SIMONE — The impact of vibration on our body and our life, in general, is very strong. We have already spoken about resonance (in the superpower you didn't know you had), but in this ritual I would like to go a little deeper and analyze how these vibrations work. Physics defines "vibration" as a mechanical oscillation about an equilibrium point and with "frequency," measured in hertz, or the number of vibrations (or, to be precise, "the number of periodic or oscillatory movements") that repeat in one second.

The whole universe has its own frequency. Back in 1952, German physicist Winfried Otto Schumann was able to calculate that the replication of DNA occurs at 8 hertz and that the rhythm of the Earth is 7.83 hertz.

Everything has its own vibration, from astronomical bodies millions of light-years away to the organs in our bodies. The brain, for example, emits Alpha waves (7 to 13 hertz) when we are relaxed but alert and waves lower than 4 hertz when we are in deep sleep.

This is where resonance comes into play. When two bodies vibrate at the same frequency, they extensively amplify the breadth of their oscillations, creating a multiplying effect. According to yoga practice, the primordial vibration of the universe is expressed through the mantra "Aum" (Om). Reciting this mantra releases a powerful frequency. The word "mantra" means "vehicle of thought," and mantras, which combine the emission of vibration and the profound meaning of the syllable, are used as both meditative and religious formulas.

Reciting a mantra works like a cure. As it vibrates inside us, it reaches and cleanses our organs and thoughts. The one I love most is *Om Mani Padme Hum*, which is an important part of Tibetan Buddhism and is dedicated to the *bodhisattva* of compassion, *Avalokiteśvara*. In the Notes, we have included where you can find some of these mantras. Try them out and harmonize, recognizing what resonates most in you. Recite it without stopping and you'll see the effects it has.

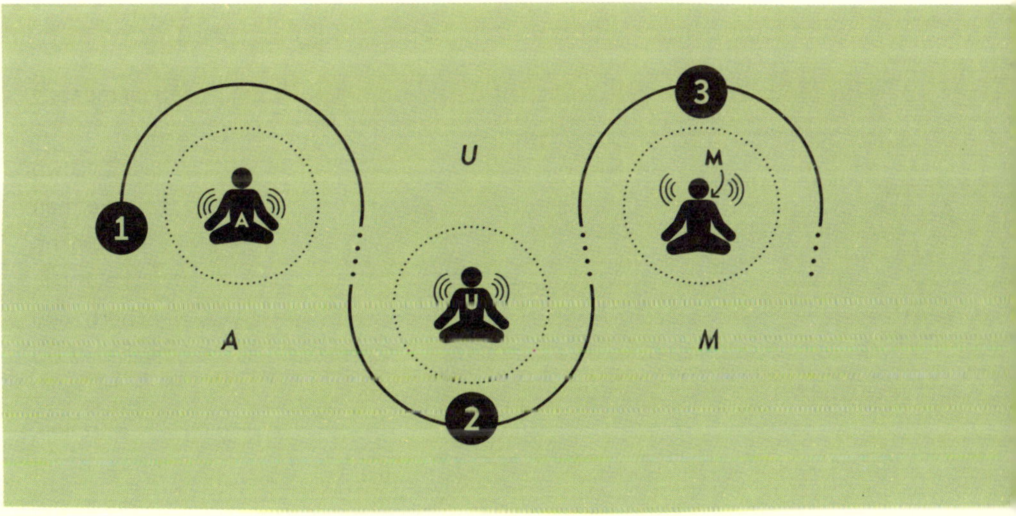

Filling Ourselves with Good Things

04

SIMONE — As you have understood by now, we are fascinated with folk culture. When proverbs and ancient stories enter our lives, we try to derive the deepest meaning from them.

Often, we find "If you sleep with dogs, you'll wake up with fleas." This metaphor is rather simple. The context we live in conditions us to the point that we risk becoming an integral part of it. This popular wisdom has a scientific counterpart: epigenetics, which was established by Conrad H. Waddington in 1942.

Epigenetics is a branch of study that looks at the changes that influence phenotype, or the genetic characteristics of an individual, without altering the genotype, or our entire DNA. In practice, it evaluates the degree to which exposure to the surrounding environment influences our genes. When I was reading about epigenetics, it struck me that the examples used to explain these influences almost always have a negative connotation. They talk about toxins, stress, trauma, and illness as things that affect us negatively from when we are embryos to when we are adults.

If epigenetics is an applied science, the opposite must also be true. Therefore, if we fill our environments with positive elements, our genes will also benefit. To simplify, let's say that if external elements have the power to raise or lower our internal energy, that means that at any moment we can choose whether what we are about to do will raise or lower the volume of our energy, like a DJ. And what about the ritual? Any time you are eating or reading or watching TV, ask yourself if this action will raise or lower your energy. In no time, you'll find yourselves noticing how many of the things you expose yourself to daily can drag you down rather than pick you up. When you do, take a final look, thank them, and then let them go because you've decided you don't need them anymore.

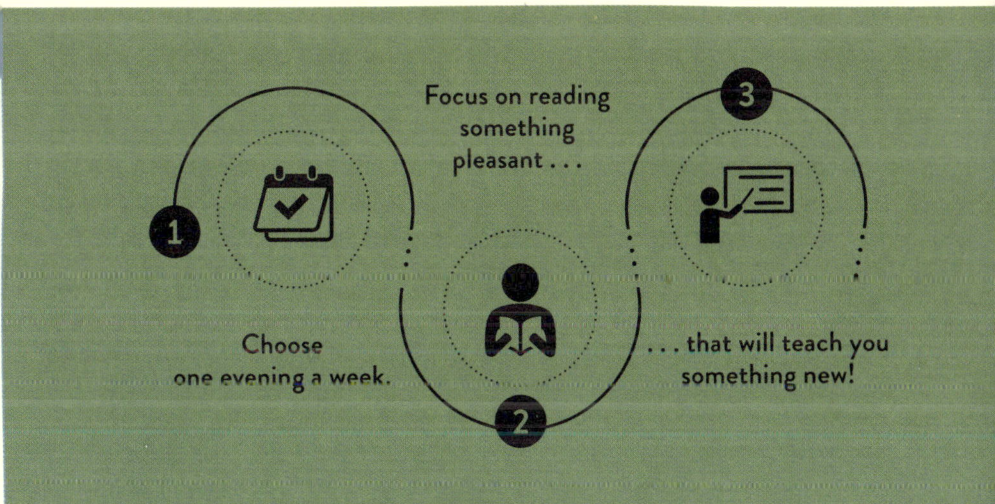

The Sound of Silence

05

FEDERICA — There are days in which I would like complete silence for 24 hours. Do you ever feel this way? No notifications, no background noise, no telephone rings, no shouting around me.

It's just silence in which I can listen carefully to myself and not load information upon information upon information. . . . Doing many things at once when too often surrounded by noise is a trap that we have unknowingly fallen into. It's called "modernity" or "multitasking." However, only with silence can we learn to sharpen other senses and perceive our own sensations.

We are so used to being immersed in auditory stimuli and noise that we often associate silence with punishment, a slightly cold state in which nothing happens. When I teach yoga, I realize how much some participants struggle when I ask them to stay silent. Florence Nightingale, the founder of modern nursing, believed that "Unnecessary noise is the most cruel absence of care that can be inflicted on the sick or the unwell." It was the end of the 1800s, but Florence already understood the toxic effect of noise. Recent studies have demonstrated that the body immediately reacts to noise, even in deep sleep, producing cortisol, the stress hormone. In large cities and very noisy places, people have much higher levels of cortisol in their blood. One study about noise conducted on mice by biologist Imke Kirste at Duke University in Durham, North Carolina, revealed to her surprise that it was not sound that stimulated the cerebral cortex but rather silence. The total absence of inputs brought more surprising results than auditory stimulation. She also found that silence stimulates the hippocampus and is an ally against dementia and depression.

And so we would like to celebrate silence and give our ears a little gift of gratitude. Let's start with 20 minutes of regenerative silence a day.

Poo Time

06

FEDERICA — Pooing is a topic that no one wants to discuss and is often considered an obviously lone moment. We preach about breathing and can even talk about peeing with some dignity, but pooing is off-limits. Perhaps that is because, since we are headed quickly toward dehumanization, we think we can resolve the problem by not facing it. We, however, love to spark reflections . . . think about how present poo is in your life. What if you can't go, can't find a bathroom, poo too much, are overcome with mental taboos and hold it in: it's the only moment a day you have to yourself!

We would like to address this matter in the simplest way possible, by asking: What is the best way to poo? There's no need to tell you that what comes out is connected to what goes in; so if your diet is off, you should pay more attention to what you eat (although, as we already mentioned, we have no intention of giving you nutrition advice. You can find your own way or a professional who can help you better). Anatomically speaking, however, we are made more or less all in the same way; therefore, there is a correct way to go to the bathroom. When we are sitting, the rectum (the final part of the intestine) bends and does not facilitate the operation, pushing waste toward the pelvic floor. Giulia Enders wrote in her famous book *Gut: The Inside Story of Our Body's Most Underrated Organ* that 1.2 billion people in the world use the squat position to poo, which has a lower risk of hemorrhoids and diverticula, whereas we continue to buy beautiful and tall toilet seats that, although aesthetically pleasing, hinder results and lead us to treat defecation as a taboo. Watch the video *Squatty Potty* on YouTube and give your intestine a bit of gratitude. The next time you go to the bathroom, offer it some relief. In addition, remember to follow your sensations, not the situation you are in when it comes to pooing. Avoid fecaliths (masses of hardened feces that are hard to expel), and you will be giving yourself the best gift ever.

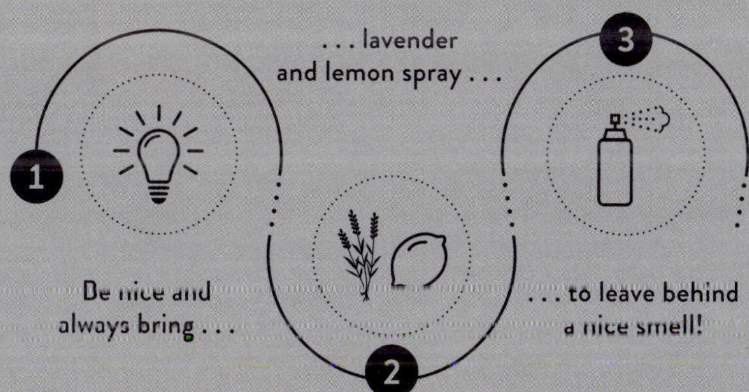

Eat When You Are Hungry, Sleep When You Are Tired

07

SIMONE — I didn't write the title, and I know for certain that many of you already knew that. The motto "Eat when you are hungry, sleep when you are tired" is one of the famous *koan* of Zen Buddhism, and there are different versions of it. What perhaps not everyone knows is that it comes from a response that a monk gave to the question of all questions: "Master, what is enlightenment?" I am very passionate about these apparently simple anecdotes that masters use to communicate deep truths, things that the rational mind is unable to understand. A true master uses these powerful tools because they know that when a student dedicates time to watching, touching, smelling, understanding with all their abilities while listening to that sentence, it leads to deeper meaning.

Don't worry, the ritual in this chapter isn't about finding an answer to the question of all questions, but rather paying attention to moments in which you can listen to yourselves. What is my body saying that I am ignoring? What is actually moving within me?

We are not accustomed to taking time for ourselves; and when we do, we naturally tend to fill every space. In art as well as psychology, the feeling at the foundation of this approach is called *Horror vacui* or kenophobia, the fear of emptiness or empty spaces. Filling spaces, often with unhealthful habits, is the exact opposite of taking care of ourselves.

Try to get rid of this tendency through two simple actions you can do every day. The first is when you head to get lunch. Ask yourself if you are truly hungry or if you are just fulfilling a habit. The second is to consider when your body really needs to rest. Instead of looking at the clock and saying that it's too early, turn off your phone and TV, brush your teeth, and simply go to bed. And if you should see the Zen monk in your sleep, thank him for having shared this Buddhist *koan* with us.

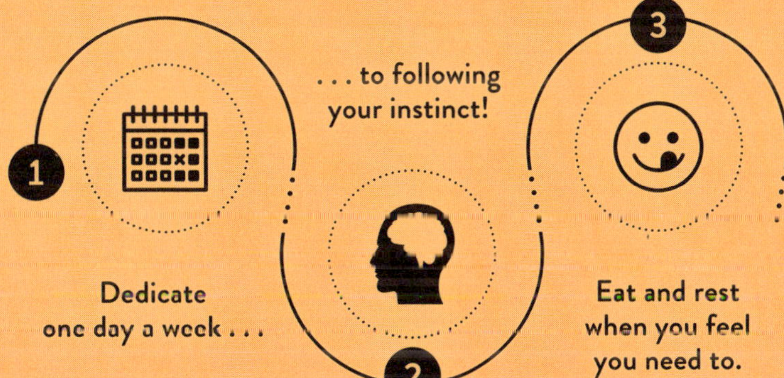

Notes and Sources

01 RECEPTIVE RECEPTORS. Start giving your spaces a smell. It's a very gratifying ritual. One of our favorite books on aromatherapy and essential oils is *My Essential Oils Bible* by Danièle Festy. We use it to create new blends as well as a sort of natural first aid kit. And praise be to Tea Tree oil!

---

02 AN OCEAN OF SENSATIONS. Test out any type of product, although we recommend focusing on natural and untreated ones. Try Epsom salts, especially if you need muscle relief. If you have a shower, buy a natural brush for dry brushing. If you want more direction, search for information about Sebastian Kniepp, an advocate of hydrotherapy.

---

03 THE SOUND THAT VIBRATES WITHIN US. If you want to listen to mantras, ones that are easy on Western ears, we recommend the album *Offering Chant* by Lama Gyurme and Jean-Philippe Rykiel. One of our favorite songs is "Medicine Buddha," a mantra for increasing the innate curative wisdom present in everyone.

---

04 FILLING OURSELVES WITH GOOD THINGS. If you want to know more about the interdependent relationship between an individual and their environment, read *The Symphony of Living: How Epigenetics Will Change Your Life* by Joël de Rosnay.

---

05 THE SOUND OF SILENCE. After all the points we have shared in this book, we suggest you courageously try finding time for a day of silence. If you can, find one of the many places that offer experiences. In Italy, one of the best is the Eremito, a former convent in Umbria that will give you a unique sense of peace and silence.

06 POO TIME. If using the bathroom when you are out makes you uncomfortable, always bring some small items for disinfecting surfaces as well as poo-drops, perfume spray (Federica loves the Aesop ones) to leave the bathroom free of bad odors. You can find different brands online or search for tutorials to make your own. This can help you overcome the embarrassment of using public bathrooms.

07 EAT WHEN YOU ARE HUNGRY, SLEEP WHEN YOU ARE TIRED. To learn more about the *koan*, and Zen in general, we recommend *101 Zen Stories* by Nyogen Senzaki and Paul Reps, a classic written in 1919 that collects *koan* from the nineteenth and twentieth centuries.

6 Green Time

In this book of gratitude, we certainly cannot forget to include a chapter about the world that sustains us. Thank you, planet Earth. This chapter is dedicated to actions that can improve the relationship we have with the environment.

We say "improve" because this topic is delicate. We don't have much time, and our ignorance (or disinterest—we're not sure which is worse) only makes the situation more difficult. According to science, the climate problem we are facing is reaching a critical point. If someone says that the studies on the risks we are taking are false or biased, tell them to take a look around. Invite them to look at the mountains—once covered in glaciers, they are now bare rock—or to dive in our oceans to verify in person the blight of our barrier reefs. Ask them to think about the persistent spread of deserts and to see for themselves how much of the surrounding landscape has been consumed.

Denying the devastating climate changes that are occurring and the fact that humans are at fault is like denying the sunrise every morning. With regard to the actual data, we suggest following Earth Overshoot Day, the date when our demand for resources each year exceeds the number of resources that the Earth can reproduce that year. To use a simpler analogy, it's the day every year that our account hits zero and we have to tap into our children's accounts to pay the bills. This day is calculated by the Global Footprint Network, an international nonprofit that has been monitoring the use of our planet's resources since 2003. It's a complex calculation, but we strongly recommend understanding how it works. In 1970, Earth Overshoot Day was December 27. In 2019, it was July 29! Stop for a second and think about this date. In order to dress, feed, care for, beautify, and entertain the almost eight billion people on Earth, we had to use resources for five months that the planet was unable to reproduce throughout the rest of 2019. Being in debt with the planet's resources for five months of the year means that after three years, we've wasted a year's worth of the planet's resources. As you can imagine, this trend is constantly and definitively worsening.

Many who have already given up hope often say "What can I do? What power do I have to change anything?" But it's 2021, and we have the Internet. It's time to be informed, act responsibly, and stop putting our heads in the sand, thinking we can't do anything. To put it more gently, we'd like to share an experience we had at the Natural History Museum of Helsinki, which we liked for its simplicity and depth. In a room dedicated to climate change, there was a phrase that suggested how we might change course in the near future. It said "Live modestly." These two words urge us to live simply and consume less.

We all want new things all the time. Maybe it's an electronic gadget, a new pair of shoes, extra comforts, a trip, etc. We live in a world that runs on a system of production and consumption, and therefore the artificial creation of needs (and products that can satisfy those needs, even if only temporarily), needs we never had before. We understand how marketing works, so we increasingly ask ourselves if it makes sense to support brands and companies when they continue to pollute the planet with their often useless products.

As for our rituals, we do not want to handle this chapter too lightly. We would like to get straight to the point and invite you to seriously change your habits. If you won't do it for yourselves or the people around you, do it for the larger sense of responsibility beyond your personal interests. Or do it to prove Agent Smith from *The Matrix* wrong. He explains to Morpheus how he came to understand that humans are not mammals—because mammals instinctively seek to live in equilibrium with the environment they live in, whereas humans multiply and exhaust resources wherever they go. Agent Smith compares us to a virus, a plague. Knowing what's happening to our planet, can we say that he's wrong?

In all this bitterness, where might we find gratitude? We think the actor, director, singer, and producer Ricky Gervais expressed it perfectly in a tweet from 2018: "We are on a rock traveling around 1 of 100 billion stars. Our species is 1 of over half a billion that have ever existed. Our chances of being born are about 1 in 400 trillion. You're not special, but you are fucking lucky. Enjoy your amazing life. You'll never exist again."

Green Guerrilla

01

FEDERICA—In a previous life, I must have belonged to a woodland community, one that has a vital relationship with plants. Because of my passion for gardening, our little city garden is an unruly jungle, home to various plants and experiments, including avocado trees, garlic plants, and others adopted for a series of reasons—like friends leaving them when moving or on vacation or when they are about to die, knowing we can't stand when plants are thrown out. Quite often, they end up staying. They are cared for, fertilized, and brought back to life.

I have always supported the Guerrilla Gardening movement and am fascinated by the work of Liz Christy and her Green Guerrillas group in New York back in 1973. They recovered a private plot of land in the city to convert it into a nurtured and public green space. Gardening is not only good for the planet and the gardener, but is also an important gesture and tribute of gratitude to the Earth. Stefano Mancuso, a botanist and author of the book *The Nation of Plants*, says that in order to change course and keep CO_2 emissions under control, we would need to plant one billion plants. That's a lot. But we have a list of Guerrilla Gardening practices you can begin with. You can start by "getting your hands dirty" and adorning your house with herbs and little succulents so that you get used to observing and understanding the rhythms of a plant. You can also create seed bombs with grasses or herbs and drop them whenever you see a sad or bare piece of land. Or you could use leftover coffee grounds to grow edible mushrooms at home or to fertilize your plants. Learn to cheerfully and randomly plant food waste, like avocado seeds, lemon seeds, fennel stalks, and celery stalks. Find experiments that make you happy!

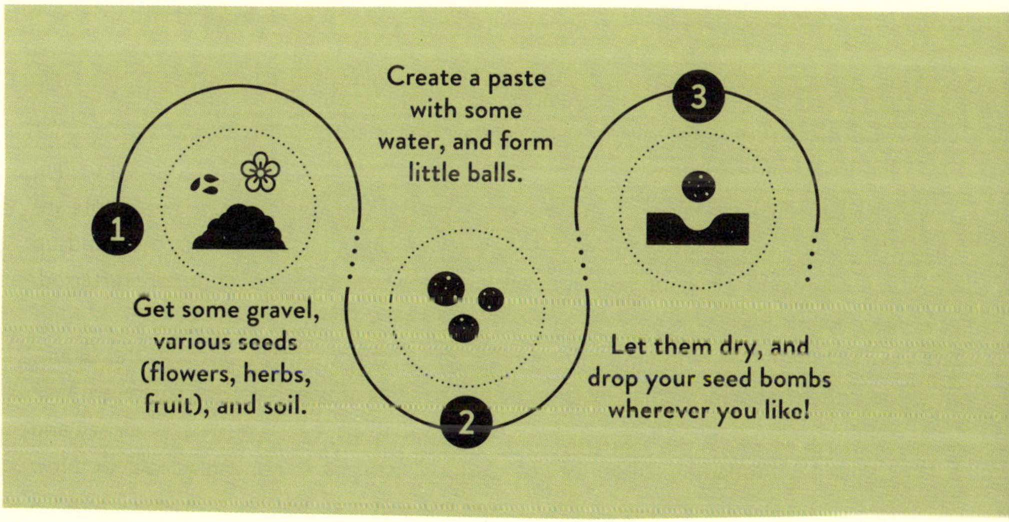

Take Care of What You Have

02

FEDERICA — One person who was fundamental in my cultural and emotional education was Zygmunt Bauman. In *Liquid Life*, which we suggest reading, and in his other books, the Polish sociologist and philosopher presents an incredibly real and vivid interpretation of the society we live in. One part that has always stayed with me is the concept of "repairing" rather than "replacing." I, like many, tend to buy a new product rather than fixing a broken one. On a macroscopic level, this process is part of a dangerous short-circuit called "consumer society." There are increasingly too many goods in circulation, a subsequent rise in the energy needed to produce them, and an increasing amount of waste we don't know how to dispose of.

Two years ago, when I was switching out my clothes for the new season, I noticed how many clothes I had accumulated over the years. Instead of packing everything away until the next season, I laid everything out and thought about each piece of clothing. How had I accumulated so much? The clothes I actually used could be counted on one hand. The rest had simply been set aside because they were too long, too big, missing buttons, or had a broken zipper. What should I sacrifice? I began to divide everything into problem categories. At the end of the day, I had a bag full of clothes in good condition to give away to friends and one full of things that needed to be repaired, adjusted, or made new again. How many things do you have—clothes, technology, or otherwise—that only need a little attention and care to take on a new life? Show some gratitude toward these objects as well as the environment. Try to fix them before buying something new.

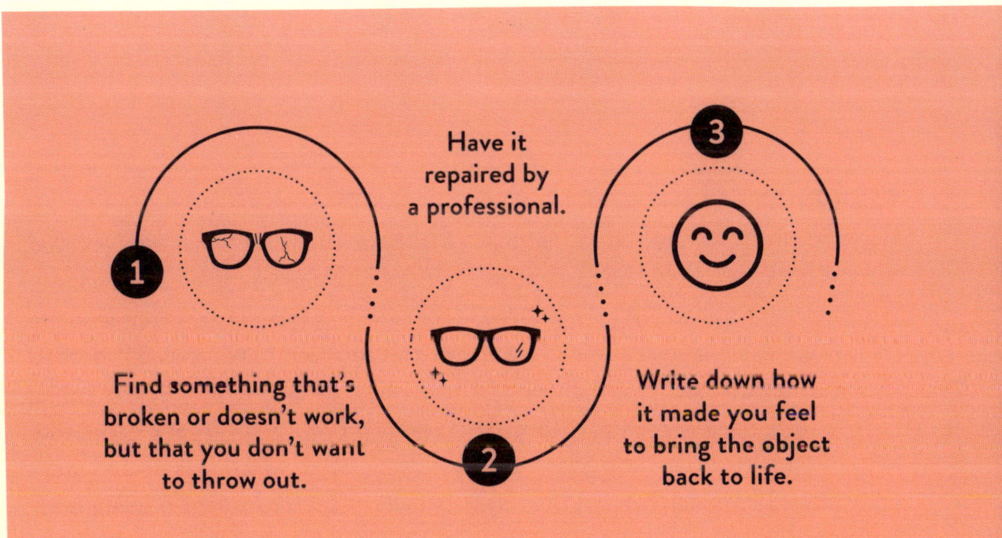

No Food Waste

03

FEDERICA — I was recently asked after finishing a meal in a famous restaurant if I would like to take home what I hadn't finished. "Would you like us to box this up so you can eat it tomorrow?" Of course, I would, thanks!

The doggy bag is growing in popularity in many countries, at least in more progressive places that support the idea of finishing your meal or wine at a later time. Think about it. You paid for it! We have used this same concept for dinner with friends. Everyone brings a container with them to take home some of the leftovers. We even did this at our wedding! Guests went home with a "wedding box," and we took home the wedding cake, which was shared with tenants in our apartment building later that evening!

Remember that 30 percent of the food ordered at restaurants and 1/3 of food produced in the world goes to waste. This is an absurd number, and each of us can do something to improve the situation! If you work in food services, try offering this possibility to your customers. Give it a creative spin, using pretty boxes that become part of the experience. If you are a customer, ask for smaller portions if you think you can't finish; ask to skip the bread and other pre-dinner snacks, which will only make you lose your appetite; share plates; and order according to how hungry you are. You can also direct restaurant owners to people or organizations who can help redistribute food. And if you leave food on your plate, proudly take a doggy bag home.

Many new initiatives work to reduce food waste and inform public opinion. This is one of the most interesting examples of how digital applications can be useful today. Always stay informed through your digital stores and check your area for new places that could help you with your goals.

Spread gratitude so that Earth's abundance is not wasted!

Activate Your Ecological Mindset

04

SIMONE — Ecology is a rather familiar term, but it's hard for us to connect it to the private sphere as if we aren't able to fully understand its meaning. See if this makes sense: Ecology means understanding the interactions between living beings and the environment they inhabit and knowing how to perceive its implications. This approach should make it easier to interpret our suggestion of activating the ecological mindset.

Something that strongly inspired me to keep these interactions alive and active is called the Eden Project, a beautiful park in Cornwall, England, where giant high-tech bubbles house tropical forests. Built in an abandoned clay pit, the park has welcomed more than 20 million visitors since 2001. It shows people how small daily acts—like transplanting a plant or growing a balcony garden—can effect real change. I am very fond of Tim Smit, one of the visionary founders of this non-profit initiative, and David Harland, its meticulous and competent guide. I owe them a huge debt of gratitude for all they taught me and the thousands of other people who visit Eden every year. It was in Cornwall that I learned about the sharing economy for the first time. The idea is to share part of your personal goods with others, especially those we use less often.

Does it make sense for two neighbors to have different power washers, something they might use three times a year? If I'm looking for a certain type of cell phone, wouldn't it be better to ask around and see if someone is no longer using one? If you love physical books, why not try a platform for exchanging books, like BookMooch? If you have an idea that fits into the sharing economy, even something small, start doing it now! Know that this is an act of gratitude toward the planet's resources. It costs nothing and will give you so much back.

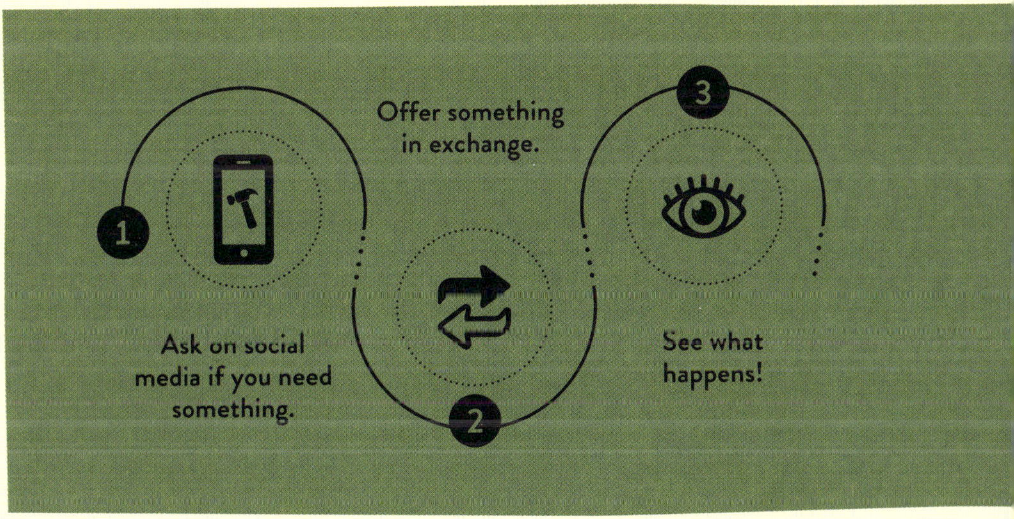

The Social Act of Commuting

05

SIMONE — I believe the act of walking is revolutionary. It's good for your physical and mental health; it allows you to discover the city, neighborhoods, and people around you; it makes me feel like I'm reclaiming the space I live in; it saves money; and above all, it reduces pollution. In my family, taking a walk has always been an important moment of togetherness, whether it's strolling through a park or walking after dinner. We also know of some organizations that make walking a symbolic tool of solidarity toward migrant populations that walk to freedom in order to escape war or famine. "Walking daily will change your vision of the world. You observe the details of places, become aware of the city's problems and those of its people. To me, this is the greatest revolution," says Paolo Piacentini, president of Federtrek, an organization of social promotion. I just had to sign up. But let's not stop here. You can also use skateboards, hoverboards, scooters, bicycles, or any electric version of these, as well as public transportation. Try to ask yourselves often: "What impact does my commute have on the environment?" Transportation is necessary, but we can transform this need into a revolutionary act of gratitude if we choose methods that respect the environment whenever we can. All you need to do is be organized or sometimes simply say "Sorry, but can we meet 30 minutes later, because I'm walking?" You will sound like a superhero, or you might just get someone to pick you up on their way, a method that would be considered part of the sharing economy—two rituals in one, magic!

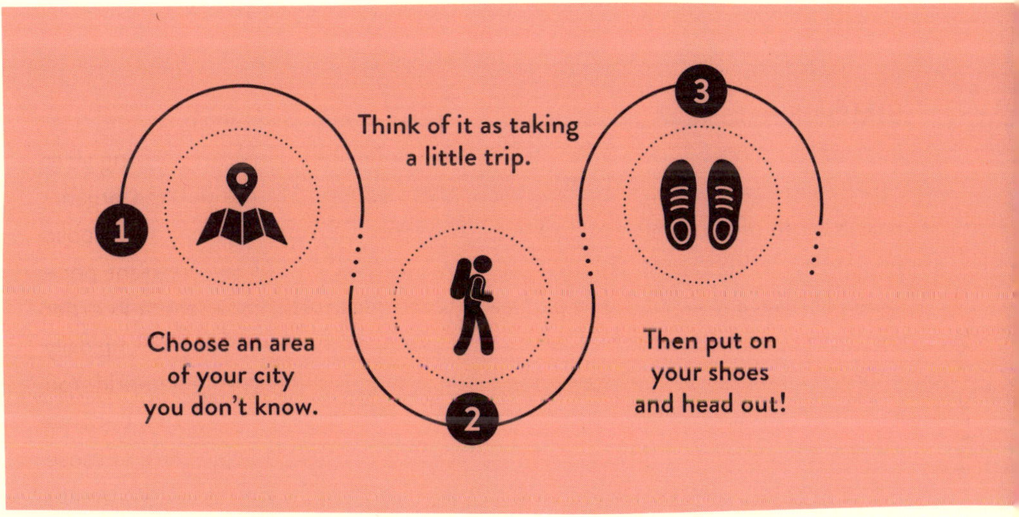

Set Your Personal Best

06

SIMONE — Those who do sports will know the expression "personal best." It refers to the best performance you can give in terms of either time or distance, depending on the sport. Runners, for example, use apps that track performances so that they can find ways to improve. Jumpers and throwers train in order to conquer a few extra centimeters and use similar methods. If you are wondering why I'm talking about sports in this chapter about the environment, it's connected to something that happened to me during the 2012 London Olympics. Every morning, I would take the subway from my hotel to the race track, and every station had large signs that said "Set a new personal best." It might have seemed like an obvious campaign for a city that was overrun by the Olympic games if it had been written by a brand connected to sports, but it was actually by Thames Water, the country's main water supply company. The company was encouraging citizens to consume less water by taking showers less than four minutes long. It was a brilliant campaign that connected the global event to a global problem, wasting water.

In the Western world, we waste an inconceivable amount of water, and if you were to start paying attention to what you consume in a day, you would be shocked. From the water you use to make coffee in the morning to the water you put in your tea at night, our days are full of moments in which we use water.

Therefore, this ritual is very simple: Use less water! It doesn't matter where or how, just try to establish a record of the least amount used every day. Every time you don't turn on the faucet or you use leftover water from washing lettuce to water your plants, give thanks. Taking water for granted is the worst mistake we can make for our future.

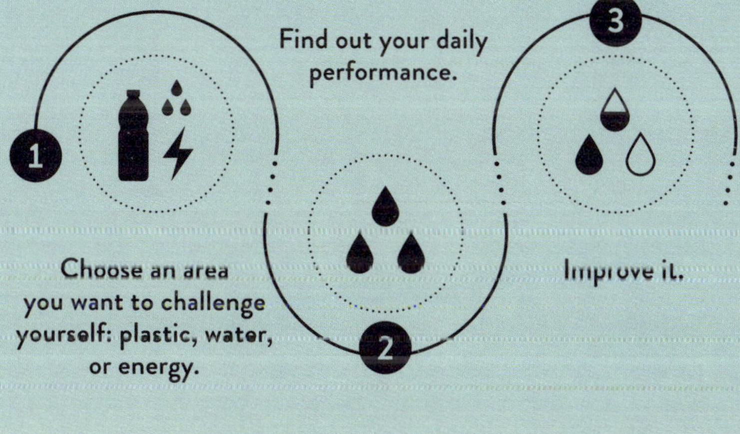

Do You Really Need It?

07

SIMONE — The rise of the digital world and social media has created a true revolution in the way we shop, even if, as we already mentioned, the number of "items" already in circulation is too high. First, we recommended fixing things before throwing them out. Here, instead, we ask you to challenge yourself to be more aware, to feed your sense of gratitude toward the planet for providing the air we breathe, the soil we use to grow food, and the water we drink. Unless you suffer from oniomania (compulsive shopping, a disorder established by the German psychiatrist Emil Kraepelin at the beginning of the twentieth century), the next time you go to buy something, ask yourself to differentiate between your emotional state and actual need. Stop for a second and think about what you are doing. This reflection will have two beneficial effects. The first is economic (Do you really need that cheap T-shirt? Are you sure you can't use that money for something that might provoke more positive emotions?) and the second is environmental (Do you know how that shirt is made? Can you read the label? Can you find the country where it was made on a map?). If after your reflection you still believe you need it, we recommend looking into theories of "degrowth" (and today, it's not at all easy) and the work of French economist and philosopher Serge Latouche. His eight Rs (Reassess, Reframe, Restructure, Re-localize, Redistribute, Reduce, Reuse, and Recycle) are listed in *Farewell to Growth*, an interesting book that can help us better define the future.

We don't want to be pessimists, but we have no reason to be optimists. Let's try to be realists and take responsibility for all our actions.

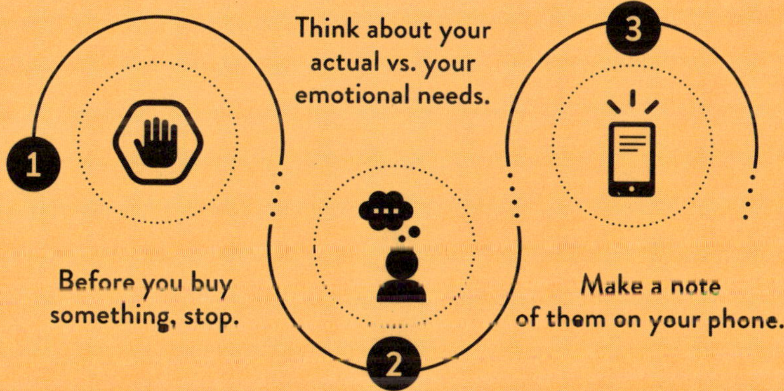

Notes and Sources

01 GREEN GUERRILLA. Stefano Mancuso is director of the International Laboratory of Plant Neurobiology, a member of the Accademia dei Georgofili in Florence, and professor of Arboriculture at the University of Florence. We aren't sure which of his books to recommend first, so start with whichever interests you most. And don't forget to monitor Earth Overshoot Day on its website.

---

02 TAKE CARE OF WHAT YOU HAVE. You can't help but love Zygmunt Bauman. We can't decide whether *Liquid Life* is a book or a sort of laical bible you should always have on hand. We would also like to recommend the documentary *Minimalism* by Joshua Fields Millburn and Ryan Nicodemus. It's interesting because it not only talks about cutting consumption but also how to consciously convert these cuts into time and money. Since understanding how it works, Federica hasn't bought new clothes for three years. She just modifies, exchanges, or converts them!

---

03 NO FOOD WASTE. Always be informed about anti-waste news. Search "waste" and "food" in your app store. You will find various types of applications on the subject. You can also become active by joining the network Social Street.

---

04 ACTIVATE YOUR ECOLOGICAL MINDSET. We recommend the book *Societing: Marketing in a Postmodern World* by sociologist Giampaolo Fabris. We also suggest checking out the project "Lulu dans ma rue," created by Charles-Edouard Vincent, teacher of social economy at HEC. The project involves virtual and physical neighborhood concierge services, which exchanges objects and services available to everyone. The rates are low, and it offers everything from searching for a service (babysitting, shopping, etc.) to requests for assistance in setting up objects. This is the social economy in which we can maximize our ecological mindset. And don't forget to go visit the Eden Project!

---

05 **THE SOCIAL ACT OF COMMUTING.** There are so many options for joining walking groups, and you don't have to start with the Camino de Santiago. Practice by walking around your city and finding others who are involved in social trekking groups in your area. You will learn about many nearby places to walk. Be curious and search for apps that suggest new ways to commute more ecologically.

---

06 **SET YOUR PERSONAL BEST.** Here are a few useful things you can do: have the thermoregulation of your home assessed, correctly adjust the temperature of your refrigerator, choose products with less packaging, and please stop buying plastic water bottles!

---

07 **DO YOU REALLY NEED IT?** Serge Latouche's book *Farewell to Growth* is fundamental and still current. Italian meteorologist and popular scientist Luca Mercalli wrote a nice book called *Prepare for a World with Fewer Resources, Less Energy, Less Abundance . . . and Greater Happiness*, which tells readers to turn off the lights but never their brains so that they are ready for our current crises—climatic, environmental, and social.

7

Bed Time

It's true, we have reached the end. Strange, huh? It feels like it was only yesterday that we timidly exchanged our first few words in an attempt to explain what rituals mean to us, where they come from, and why the number seven is important to us.

Now, around 130 pages and many beautiful illustrations later (thanks, Riccardo!), we have come to the good-byes (or more like "see you soon"). It was a wonderful journey, joining each other from one ritual to the next, one tradition to another. Some rituals might have struck you more than others, and that's okay. More than anything, we hope that you are proud of yourselves for what you have done and that you are now more familiar with your new superpower, gratitude. The more we use it, the more it grows, like experience or intelligence.

This is the exact feeling we should have when we reach the end of the day. This feeling of accomplishment, of having had new experiences—some more edifying than others—and of having learned something new. Our days come and go, and we often take them for granted, and, as you know, we have an allergic reaction when things that happen are not valued. However, our days quite often end without much fanfare.

How often do you fall asleep on the sofa with the TV on, or move from the final email of the day straight to the pillow in less than a minute, after a quick toothbrushing and trip to the bathroom? Or perhaps you return home after a night out with friends and completely forget that your toothbrush exists, leading to a difficult wakeup call the next morning (did you know that cleaning your tongue with water and lemon doesn't work miracles?).

The moment when we go to bed is important and perhaps the most ignored moment of the day of all those we've discussed. We all probably vaguely remember when our parents would put us to bed as children. Federica tells the story of when her father, a traveler, would return home and bedtime became a party full of bedtime stories with characters invented on the spot, like in improvised stand-up comedy. Simone, on the other hand, remembers it as a Pavlovian response. The end of dinner meant the end of the TV news, and that was the signal to get ready for bed, no need for other directions. This ritual is similar to the one Paolo Conte, the unmatched singer and poet, described in 2010 upon his release of *Nelson*, a record of original songs named after his dog who had recently passed away. Conte tells the story of his bedtime ritual. Before going to sleep, he would "dust off the piano keys," and this nightly concert always ended, for superstitious reasons, with a specific little tune. Curled up under the piano, Nelson would know this meant the day was over, get up, and go to sleep. Nelson was a lucky dog. For years, his nightly ritual consisted of a personal concert by one of the greatest contemporary jazz composers.

What rituals do you have for the evening? Do you have any? In this chapter, we will talk about a few that you can try out and perhaps adapt to your needs. As with all the other chapters, our main goal is to share an experience that will spark your curiosity, help you find new good habits, and show you how easy it is to transform involuntary actions into moments of awareness. We'd like to think we have given you ideas about how to find a greater connection with yourselves, your bodies, and your souls, and to feel deeply grateful to be where you are at this very moment.

So, why is getting ready for bed so important? Sleep, as we know, is the moment in which we leave the world of consciousness so that the world of unconsciousness might do some tidying up. And it's a shame to enter this state of (apparent) abandonment without being aware of the miracle of it. The moment we cross over the bridge from awake to asleep has some similarities to death. One second we are present, and a second later we are elsewhere. It is a magical moment that we should pay more attention to and for which we should be as prepared as possible. This moment prepares you for the magic of sleep, a biological miracle that helps our bodies regenerate, our rational mind calm down, and our soul finally find room to stretch its legs.

We hope that these final seven rituals inspire you to give sleep the space it deserves, because, as this first ritual says, "There is no certainty of tomorrow."

There Is No Certainty of Tomorrow

01

SIMONE — If you read the title and wondered if it was a quote from Lorenzo de' Medici, you are correct! In his poem *Canzona di Bacco* from 1490, Lorenzo The Magnificent urged others to live in the moment, enjoying everything the present offers because, again, tomorrow is not promised. For this ritual, however, we have decided to play an unexpected hand and share further information about the concept of karma, which we introduced in chapter 4. Remember that "karma" means action, and, to quote the Buddha, every action has a consequence that we will sooner or later experience, for good or for bad (or neutral, but this is another, longer story). Now, when we go to bed in the evening, we naturally reset some but not all things from the day. Our body is restored and regenerated; but if we left the dinner dishes to be washed, the next morning we will be trying to make coffee amidst a mess of pots from the night before. Dirty pans are a nice metaphor for the things we leave unfinished and will find in the same spot the next morning. In the eighteenth century, Benjamin Franklin, one of the Founding Fathers of the United States, urged people to not put off what could be done today. And this is very similar to the concept of karma. Whatever we don't face today will be waiting for us tomorrow. Often the things we put off are those that we like least, more difficult, or require more energy.

So, what is the ritual? It's simple. Understand what practical things you absolutely must finish before the end of the day (you have the honor and duty of writing your own personal list) and then don't go to sleep without having handled them. At first, this might seem tiring and might mean working overtime, but you will find that your effort will be abundantly repaid by the sense of gratitude you will feel as you lay your head on your pillow knowing that tomorrow is truly a new day.

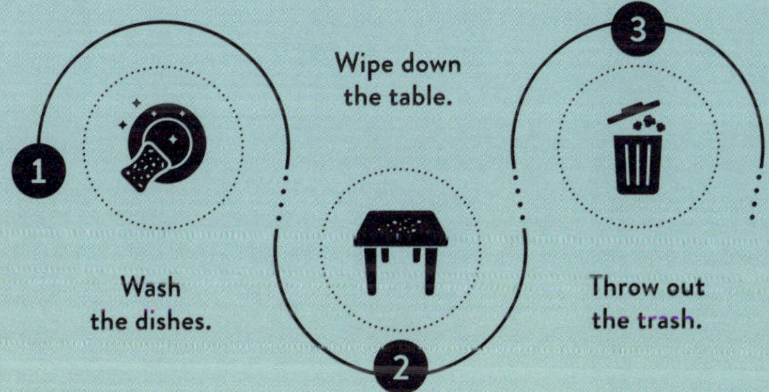

Dim the Lights

02

FEDERICA — Sunrise, sunset, dawn, and twilight might seem like simple, obvious words, but not everyone knows exactly what they mean. They are optical-astronomical phenomena regarding the light of the sun in relation to the Earth. Sunrise and sunset refer to the first and the last rays of visible light that appear, whereas dawn and twilight are the phases just before sunrise and just after sunset. Twilight is my favorite hour of the day. Whether it's winter or summer, twilight soothes me. I like to celebrate the soft blending from day to night with small gestures that help me prepare for this final part of the day. I lock the door, turn off my phone, light a candle and incense, and, most importantly, dim all the lights . . . long live bedside lamps and adjustable lights! The day has now ended, but we try to recreate a moment of transition from the full light of day to the absence of light at night. Whenever we aren't able to do so, Simone and I struggle to relax.

Every evening after sunset in Varanasi, India, Ganga Aarti, a ritual dedicated to the Ganges, is celebrated near the temple of Kashi Vishwanath. It is one of the most evocative and spectacular ceremonies in the world. The sound of a shell horn, which is one of Vishnu's four weapons and represents the object that harnessed the primordial sound of creation, signals several Hindu priests to give thanks to the river and banish negative energy from the day with fire and incense. We don't need to blow into shells or imitate the sacred rites of a specific culture. However, we, our homes, and our hearts should show gratitude toward the light of day as it leaves the Earth, and they deserve a calming ritual.

Unbuckle Your Seatbelts

03

FEDERICA— In our home, there are yoga mats everywhere (as well as myofascial balls, foam rollers, elastic bands, bolsters, etc.). I work so much with the body as both a teacher and a professional with my fingers in too many pots. With time and age, I have had to learn to pay closer attention to the rehabilitation of my muscle tissues, microtraumas, and muscle pains. For a long time, I was mostly focused on physical performance, and my age meant I wasn't open to the concept of calm. During this time, I always thought the most important thing was to exercise. But today, after personal experiences and several accidents, I am certain that movement, which is a sign of life, should always be followed by rehabilitation, rest, and stretching. It's especially important in the evening just before going to bed where you spend a lot of time lying down. A healthy back is the best gift you can give yourself, and by "healthy" I mean not just free of pain (and I beg you from the bottom of my heart, if you have any problems, please deal with them immediately) but also of minor postural soreness. So, how might you show gratitude to your back for having carried you around, supported you, and helped spread energy to the rest of your body? First of all, take a look at your mattress and think about investing in a high-quality one. It is after all where you spend, in the best of cases, a third of your day. You can also do simple stretching for your back and shoulders before going to bed, using Yin or Restorative yoga positions. You can find tutorials on YouTube, like those of Travis Eliot (You can even do them on the sofa while you watch TV!)

Lastly, we suggest finding comfort! Get rid of the jeans, belts, shoes, make-up, and contact lenses. Make these actions little gifts of wellbeing for the evening.

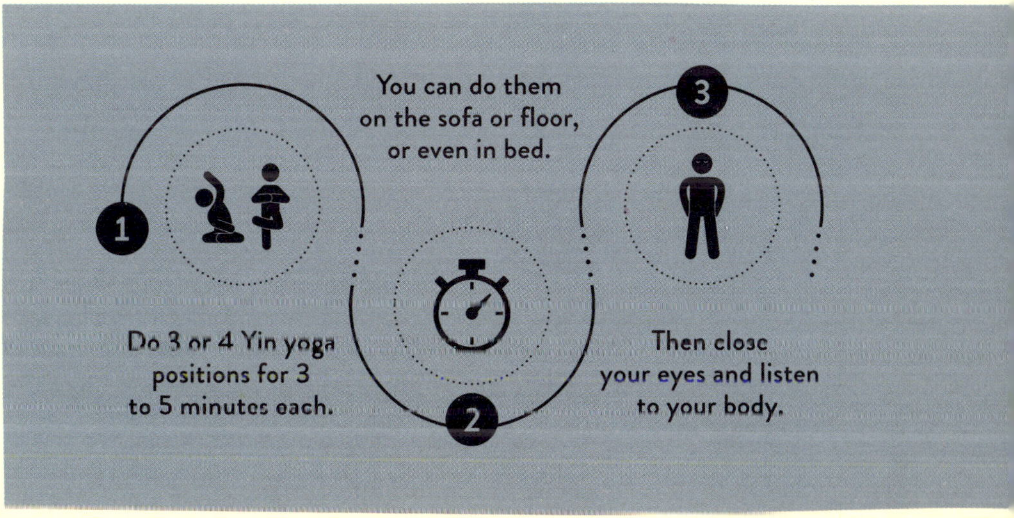

A Spoonful of Herbs

04

FEDERICA—As I already mentioned in the chapter on food, I am not a huge fan of dinner. However, this doesn't mean that when I do have dinner, I don't enjoy it. Of course, as you know, going to sleep too full and maybe a little tipsy isn't good for your sleeping or waking up the next day. We, however, have two tricks that offer a little help with digestion: our lifesaving herb, and the liquor Amaro Svedese. The herb is called Taneda (also Erba Iva or Achillea Moscata), which I've known for years because it's typical of the mountain area where I've always spent my summers, near Bormio, which is home to the classic liquor Braulio, which uses Taneda as a main ingredient. The delicate flowers of this plant grow at altitudes between 1,500 and 3,000 meters. The intense stimulating property of the flowers helps with the secretion of gastric juices, and therefore favors digestion. If we are out, we always bring a little with us in tea filters and ask for hot water after dinner to steep them in. Often, everyone around us wants to try! We should warn you, though, that it's a bitter herb, so add some honey if you don't like it. When we are at home, we always put some Amaro Svedese in hot water after dinner. Despite the name, it is not a liquor but rather a tincture. The recipe contains 21 herbs, and some believe it was created by Paracelsus, a Swiss physician, alchemist, and botanist from the Renaissance era. It was then rediscovered by two Swedish physicians, Urban Hjärne and Claus Samst, in the seventeenth century, and later revived by Maria Treben in the twentieth century in her book *Health from God's Garden*. A spoonful in a cup of hot water is our nightly ritual that helps us get ready for bed. Try out this little gesture of warm gratitude before sleeping and you will help your body more gently handle digestion.

The Night Air

05

FEDERICA — Every evening has its own smell. Summer evenings smell like hot air, citronella, and honeysuckle. Fall evenings are crisp, whereas winter is chilly. And spring smells sweet! Do you know what one of the most important things for sleep is? Temperature. In the evening, our body temperature naturally starts to lower, reaching a minimum while sleeping. This means that to sleep better, we need fresh air, and we feel this need the most in the summer, but the "fresh" air from air conditioning is not good for our health at all. Although things like coffee, alcohol, and smoking might seem like they help us relax, they are stimulants and vasodilators and will introduce a higher level of energy to our systems, and therefore are equally bad for our health. I am naturally cold, so I don't feel the same need as Simone to sleep with the window open even in winter. To avoid discussing the completely subjective topic of temperature perception, we decided to resolve this difference by dividing our duvets so that each of us can use ours as we like. However, one small but effective way to show gratitude toward your sleep is to ventilate your bedroom at least an hour before sleeping. Open your windows and let the air in. If you want to do even more, welcome the night with gratitude by turning on an essential oil diffuser with lavender. Fresh air that smells of lavender will surely make your sleep more pleasant. And if you want to intensify this ritual and tune your body to the lavender-scented energy, try to involve the people around you, like your children, partners, or roommates. You will find that the night air is calmer and more peaceful.

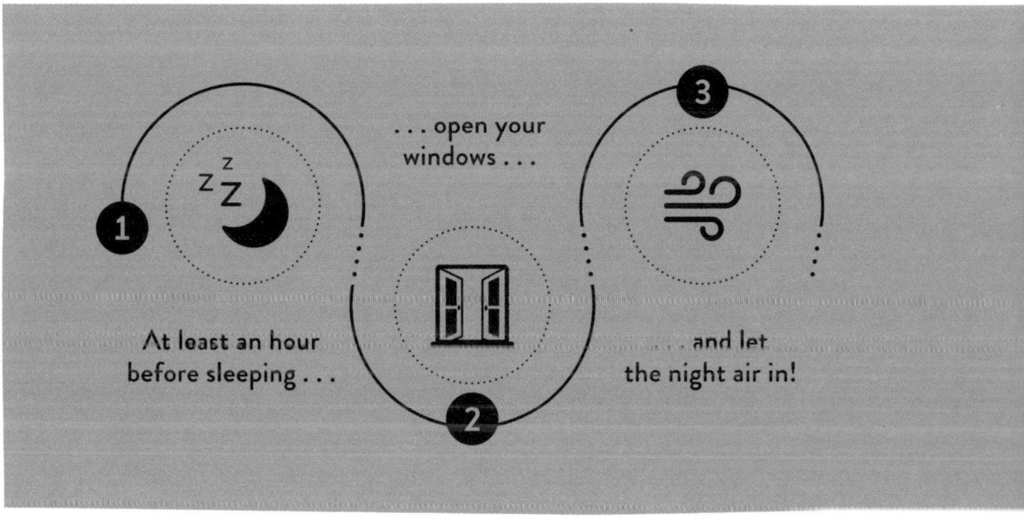

Best of the Day

06

SIMONE— "Do or not do, there is no try," said Master Yoda in *Star Wars*. If we think about it, the day that has passed is full of doing or not doing what we had imagined. Often, we find ourselves ruminating over what we could have done or couldn't do or say, and this feeling fuels the nonstop stress we have experienced throughout the day. As if that weren't enough, add to it the feelings of guilt, the "buts" and "thens," and the "This happened, but I should have done this." We hope this ritual will help you leave behind this binary, which always makes us feel unaccomplished. Lie down on the bed and think of the good moments of the day for a few minutes, like the coffee you drank in the warm sunshine, the telephone call with a nice client, the pretty drawing your child gave you, that article that fascinated you, or hitting every green light on your way home. Every day, even the darkest one, carries something sweet. Maybe it's just something very small. We would like for you to focus on these moments and dedicate your gratitude to them with a prayer. Yes, we know, in the Western world, the word "prayer" always makes us panic, for one reason or another. Prayers perhaps sound like old practices or too superstitious, but we have no problem reaffirming our strict secularism. So, don't judge them, simply find the words you want to use to say thanks.

Thanks, Tuesday, for allowing me to find that last cookie in the bottom of the box I thought was empty. Thanks, Thursday, for not having given me a fine even though I parked in the wrong spot. It's not about saying a prayer that asks for something, but rather developing a song of gratitude from the bottom of your heart for what you have already received.

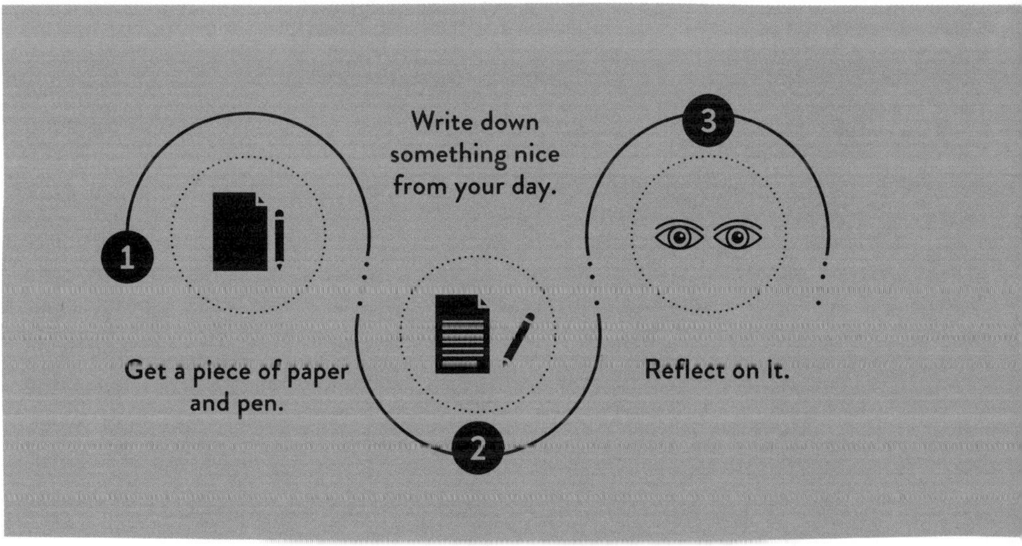

So Long, and Thanks for All the Fish

07

SIMONE — Do you remember *The Hitchhiker's Guide to the Galaxy* by Douglas Adams? You might not know that the book came from the transposition of a radio theater series on the BBC in 1978. For years, I've believed that if I were to listen to the original version, it would expand my knowledge. I'll have to remind myself again in the future.

The title of this final ritual had to recall the message of gratitude the dolphins leave behind for Earth before it is destroyed to make way for a hyperspace bypass. In the past 20 years, the expression has been adopted as a common way to say good-bye among fans of the book, including us.

I don't think the Tibetan monks in the Himalayan caves know Adams, but every evening before going to bed, they do something similar. They get their bowl, the only object they own, and, after emptying it, they put it face-down. They don't do it to prevent bugs from getting inside during the night but rather as a symbolic gesture that means they would be ready to die that night and that they've left nothing unfinished. It is a very simple gesture but one of extreme consciousness. They are stating that they are ready to leave their bodies, knowing that they have taken care of every debt or credit. Don't worry, this final ritual won't betray the very real spirit of all the suggestions we've shared so far. We won't ask you to do anything that would possibly be meaningless for anyone who, like us, hasn't decided to dedicate their lives to meditation. It is, however, a similarly simple action. When you turn off the light, when you literally pass from light to dark, do so with all the awareness you can muster. Make sure you focus all your attention on these actions you've been doing your whole life, and as you pass from the light to the dark, say a huge thanks to the universe. The universe will pay you back in the same way, affectionately.

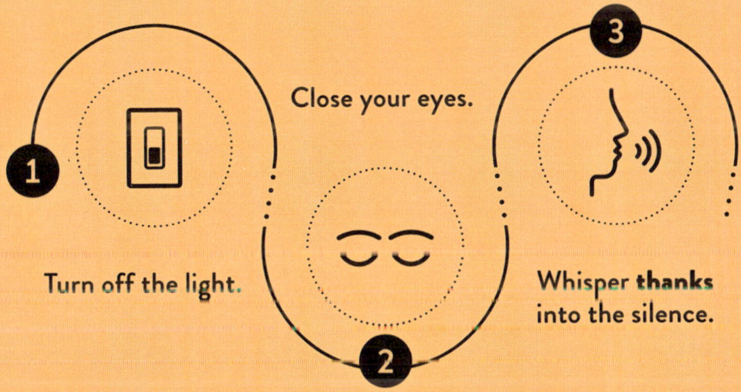

Notes and Sources

01 THERE IS NO CERTAINTY OF TOMORROW. We find methods based on to-do lists vaguely anxiety-inducing and already looking too far into the future. Stay here, in the present day that's coming to a close, and focus on finishing something that would frustrate you if you were to find it in front of you tomorrow morning. These should be small, concrete things that train the soul for tomorrow's more demanding challenges.

---

02 DIM THE LIGHTS. Fire and light are powerful elements. Keep a candle in your house and watch it in the dim light of a room. Let your thoughts from the day go, without judgment. Or light some incense. We love the sandalwood scent from Nippon Kodo or Tibetan incense, which burns without the wooden center, diffusing subtle but evocative fragrances.

---

03 UNBUCKLE YOUR SEATBELT. Travis Eliot is one of my favorite masters, especially for his ability to popularize Yin yoga. I recommend reading his book *A Journey into Yin Yoga*. Today, we pay little attention to the energy of our yin side, not only when we talk about movement but in general. Without getting into the energy theories of Taoism, this discipline is for everyone because it has you work on the deeper levels of your physical structure and invites you to "let go" rather than do.

---

04 A SPOONFUL OF HERBS. If you don't have a local herbalist shop, you can try products from Pukka Herbs. Two of our favorite blends are one made with chamomile, licorice, and fennel, and one with three types of chamomile (Egyptian, European, and African). It is a warm treat to sip on the sofa.

---

05 THE NIGHT AIR. Your mattress and pillow are not things you need to save on. If you have to buy one, do a lot of research and choose one that doesn't get hot and is dual-season! For couples, we suggest doing what we did: different mattress-es, because we all have different needs and we all deserve sweet dreams.

06 BEST OF THE DAY. Choose a nice notebook with a cover and texture you like to look at and feel. Place it in a convenient spot next to the bed. Let your heart speak freely as you take notes with simple words, drawings, or sentences.

07 SO LONG, AND THANKS FOR ALL THE FISH. If you don't have a nightstand or easy-to-reach light for this moment, use LED string lights that you can find at Ikea. We have them wrapped around our bed to create dim light that can easily be turned off. They also don't need electricity, just batteries.

Acknowledgments

Do you really want to spend time reading the names of people you don't know? Probably not. That's why we decided to create a new ritual.

It works like this. Once this book is published, we are going to go knock on the doors of all the people who made this book possible. We will dress nicely, put on our best smile, bring a small gift in the shape of a book with a bow (whatever could be inside?), and when the door opens, we will tell each person, from the bottom of our hearts, "Thank you."

P.S. Even if you haven't written a book, if you think this ritual could be as useful as the others, don't hesitate to use it. Put on your best smile, knock on the doors of all the people who have supported, loved, and pushed you as well as rejoiced with you, those people who are fundamental in your life, and tell them

THANK YOU.

FEDERICA AVANZI was a creative and strategic director at Italian and foreign publishers and broadcasters for 12 years. She is also a digital humanist, teacher, and speaker in digital and social communication, as well as an author and Pilates and yoga instructor. She borrows tools from the world of communications to help teach her students, and techniques from the world of holism to make her communication more caring and coherent.

Today she focuses on studying the psychology of yoga as she continues to work as a business partner in the field of sustainable economics and digital innovation. She dreams of living barefoot in the grass in a place where she can create a work studio and retreat.

SIMONE MASSERINI is an executive director and has guided people and designed projects in the world of sports, entertainment, and corporate businesses for 20 years. He is a mental coach, university professor, Tarot of Marseille reader, and passionate about astrology. Since 2002, he has been focused on studying Tibetan Buddhist philosophy at the Karmapa International Buddhist Institute of New Delhi. His curiosity and adventurous spirit have led him to spend long periods of time abroad, from India to Brazil, France to Cornwall, Scotland to Mexico.

Today, he has found the right balance between his professional life—focusing on helping companies, teams, and projects find the right nuance in increasingly complex markets—and his continuous and unorthodox spiritual search. When he wants to know what the future will bring, Simone asks The Sandman, Neil Gaiman's lord of dreams. After reading *The Inn at the End of the World*, every time he arrives somewhere new, he looks around for signs of the centaur Chiron having passed through.

RICCARDO GOLA is an illustrator, graphic designer, art director, and musician. He worked as an art director in various advertising agencies for years and has now been a graphic designer, illustrator, and art director with PEPE nymi for 10 years, where he mostly works on book covers. He has designed covers for many publishers, including Rizzoli, Garzanti, Amazon Publishing, Vallardi, and Longanesi.

In recent years, his work as an illustrator has picked up, although he continues to work professionally as a jazz contrabassist and bassist.

My Rituals of Gratitude

My Rituals of Gratitude

2 1 3

2
1
3